Digital Finance, Bits and Bytes

Vasant Chintaman Joshi

Digital Finance, Bits and Bytes

The Road Ahead

palgrave
macmillan

Vasant Chintaman Joshi
General Manager (Retd.)
Bank of India
Pune, Maharashtra, India

ISBN 978-981-15-3430-0 ISBN 978-981-15-3431-7 (eBook)
https://doi.org/10.1007/978-981-15-3431-7

This Palgrave Macmillan imprint is published by the registered company Springer Nature Singapore Pte Ltd.
The registered company address is: 152 Beach Road, #21-01/04 Gateway East, Singapore 189721, Singapore

This book is dedicated to my wife
Mrs. Sulabha Joshi,
My friend, philosopher, and guide

Preface

Ever since the financial crisis [2008–2010] developed and the rescue operations began, the rescue and subsequent developments as a field of study had exerted a tremendous pull and had drawn me to the study of the subject. Earlier the 1998 SE Asian crisis and its aftermath had been a subject of lectures I delivered at Management Institutes and I kept up with my studies through books like Robert Rubin's fascinating autobiography [*In an Uncertain World*]. The problems that were dealt with and the complexities of arriving at solutions through trying political situations were fascinating fields of study. Of interest were the ways in which these situations were finally resolved.

Since 1971, when I took over the enormous responsibility for preparing and implementing the manpower plans for my bank during a very tumultuous period [post nationalization period], I had the job of providing not only the required trained manpower but to involve the operating units in execution of the tasks which the Government of the day, as owners, had posed before the banks. On the one hand, banks and the operating units had to carry on the servicing of existing customers but in the same breath take over activities never done before. This part of the process affords a unique challenge to planners and managers. The bigger the task the greater are the complexities you are called on to handle.

It is this pull which draws me to the study of a wider subject like E-Finance. The subject as would be clear to any reader is the current challenge before the financial services industry. Barely had they settled down to a new routine when they were called upon to implement and carry out an enormous change in the management task. There are social, political, and other challenges shaking up the very basic premise on which the FIs had been building up the edifice so far. Suddenly President Trump and politicians with similar ideologies reversed course and raised the "America First" banner. In Europe the groups cried hoarse against anti-immigration policies and UK decided to break away from the European Union. In countries like Italy and France there was a clamor for anti-immigration policies. The world economic order had to change gears. The global supply chains were likely to be snapped and industries were under pressure to bring back to the home countries the industries set up in different parts of the world due to cost considerations. In the alternative they had to forego the cost advantages and face the tariff regime coming in.

At the same time, on the technology front FIs had to deal with a new threat posed by the FinTechs. They became potential disruptors and began to attack the soft underbelly. They started grabbing profitable segments and that too at a time when income from the credit portfolio was on the downward side. The field for study was very wide and had already attracted a number of students, practitioners, academics, consultants, management gurus, and technology innovators. Newer aspects were being put under the scanner and some newer problems came to light. I too got attracted to the study because, for a person who spent a better part of his banking career in the field of planning and development, these areas afforded a rich field for study.

Someone who undertakes a study without the support of an academic body or department colleagues and access to experts for illuminating or guiding one's faltering footsteps is an enormous task. But if one persists and moves on, a way can be found. Obviously, one has to depend on one's children, former colleagues, associates, and other like-minded persons for getting over the various hurdles that one has to cross.

No doubt, I incurred an enormous debt of obligations and to express thanks to all of those who encouraged me and prodded me on would be too long and yet would have gaping holes. Yet, a few names have to be mentioned. At the top of the list are my daughter Achala, and my son-in-law Kirtikumar Deshpande. They spared no pains and even took on themselves the enormous task of typing and retyping my various drafts and ensured that the time schedule was strictly adhered to. I just don't have words enough to thank them. My son Vinay and his wife Neelima have always been critical analysts of my work and ensured that there was no drift or unnecessary deviations from the broad theme. Additionally, they had the enormous burden of looking after me. Great thanks are due to them.

Mr. P.B. Kulkarni, former Chairman of Bank of Maharashtra and Executive Director of Reserve Bank of India, was a constant source of encouragement. Equally important was the opportunity to discuss and seek clarifications from him whenever the need arose. My colleagues working with the Gokhale Institute of Politics and Economics were generous in their support and did not mind my troubling them not only at odd times but with equally odd requests. Advocate Pingle set aside very important work to peruse the draft on IT Acts and relevant provisions.

I must, before concluding, mention a silent supporter, guide, and philosopher who bore with me in my pursuit of endeavors for over fifty-eight years of our married life. Her insistence on simplification and clarification of complex issues, a disciplined approach to completion of tasks, and accepting the obvious in not claiming that something great is being done. Her insistence on never losing that sense of proportion has been of enormous importance. I dedicate this book to her memory and unforgettable guidance imbibed over a period of time. No words can express what I feel and yet her unspoken support molding the contours of this book is of very great value.

Finally, my editors have been patient beyond the call of their duty. The book owes a lot to their patient plodding and insistence. The mistakes and errors are, of course, mine. There are no excuses for lapses creeping in. They took a great non-insurable risk since I was already 87 years old when I started working on this book.

In the next section I give a brief chapter-wise summary for the benefit of readers so that they have before them the totality in view.

The book is broadly divided in three very broad sections. The first section takes note of the socio-economic developments and the changing environment. The next four chapters broadly describe the way FIs cope with the problems created by disruption and other environmental factors. Also, added to these changes are technology changes involved in the digitization process. Problems relating to HR management, Marketing of services, and so on are dealt with separately as they involve some discussion which covers practices to be followed.

The next three sections cover cyber-risks and normal business risks, and ways to manage them. Finally, we deal with the regulatory aspects and touch on newer approaches based on behavioral science inputs.

We conclude by saying that the author alone is responsible for the errors and omissions.

Our profuse thanks to the editorial staff at Palgrave Macmillan. But for their patient goading the book would have never been brought out.

Pune, India
20 June 2019

Vasant Chintaman Joshi

Contents

List of Figures

List of Tables

CHAPTER 1

A Brief Review: Socio-Economic Changes

Introduction

The term digital finance immediately brings to mind a marriage of complex electronics/software/computer technology and financial products. This topic is much broader in scope and its study requires a multifaceted holistic analytical approach. In this book we cover all these factors to present the reader with a comprehensive picture—starting with the socio-economic factors in the last decade that led to the growth of this field to the developments in the fields of artificial intelligence and the evolving legal/regulatory framework to deal with the developments.

It must be mentioned that the Financial Services Industry (FSI) was gradually stabilizing after the 2008–2010 crisis. It was at this stage that certain basic socio-economic policies underwent a radical change. Coupled with such changes, the technology developments made the tasks extremely difficult for them particularly in the USA.

In our discussions, we will give examples or provide information about the experiences or developments in various countries. This is primarily due to the fact that this is a rapidly evolving field and no country provides a unique answer about the various developments. The reader who, in all likelihood, is primarily leading the team involved in planning for the digital future of his organization will find that the answer lies in a thorough study of these aspects with a special focus on factors unique to his country/organization.

It is likely for example, that a senior executive of a Public Sector Indian Bank may be more worried about the issue of Non-Performing Assets and

V. C. Joshi, *Digital Finance, Bits and Bytes*,
https://doi.org/10.1007/978-981-15-3431-7_1

the possible write-downs than the problem of crimes committed using connected devices such as mobile phones and the issues of computer resource loads and balancing with the advent of Internet of Things (IoT). Such an attitude would be dangerous as the nature of digital/electronic transactions lends them to exponential growth and in a short order what appears to be a trickle of a few thousands turns into a flood of millions. The example of mobile phones and their rapid acceptance in countries where a landline telephone was a luxury only a few years back is a good example of this phenomenon.

To give an overview of our analysis in this book, we start with the socio-economic conditions in the Western countries that led to several developments and significant changes in the working and regulations of Financial Institutions. We follow that with a comprehensive review of the various technologies, the Internet and associated developments. Next, we review the impact of these technologies on Banks, Insurance companies and Brokers. A thorough look at the various cyber-laws, crimes, and the associated risk management is followed by a discussion on the overall risk management practices and developments. We study the impact of all these developments on Human Resource management and how the operations and marketing function will evolve. The final chapter will review the changing regulatory scenarios for Financial Institutions.

How it Got Here

During the last ten years, the Financial Services Industry was caught in a great flux. No doubt, part of it happened because of indiscriminate investments and excessive borrowings. Had it not been for a massive pumping in of funds (tax payers' money), the industry could not have even survived. A great catastrophe was averted because of this timely intervention by the Governments and Central Bankers. True it is, that the institutions were saved. Serious students of the financial scene have raised doubts about the efficacy of such methods in the long run. Their main complaint is that it is not certain that such measures benefit the "real" economy! Questions like "Could only some parts like affording protection to the depositors have been more useful?" have no easy answers. We must, however, add that no government can allow the majority of Financial Institutions to be crippled.

The crisis that enveloped the industry took many by surprise. It is indeed unbelievable for an industry which had a great deal of stability and a very stable business model. Its customer base was very well nursed and many of them were known to the banks/insurance companies through their association going over generations. The author distinctly remembers a function which he chaired to felicitate customers having their accounts with the bank from 1908 to 1983. Some of them proudly announced that their accounts existed when the chairman at the meeting was not even born. Perhaps, the bankers of those days were known not only for their functional specialization but also for their "family physician" like position. It, therefore, came as a rude shock when the very existence of the financial industry was in question and the trust relationship built over a period of time was blown to pieces.

The Financial Services Industry went through a very difficult period during the years 2008–2010. It would not be wrong to say that had it not been for the massive support extended by the Governments and Central Banks there could have been a systemic collapse. There was a certain price to be paid for the assistance extended. The regulators wanted the Banks/ Financial Institutions (FIs) to adhere to certain capital norms, and also strictly to adhere to quantitative restrictions on activities. Banks were also required to review their Risk Management practices, Corporate Governance systems, Bonus and Reward systems, to name only a few. In a sense these changes cold easily be initiated and completed since the steps required to be taken were solely within their own "jurisdiction" and very much under their control.

The banks and insurance companies were faced not merely with regulatory and compliance rules but it was also becoming clear that there were equally complex and important issues that had to be handled before there could be a semblance of normalcy. One of the issues of great significance for Financial Institutions pertains to the customers' loss of trust in the Financial Services Industry and to an extent even in the wider social ethos. The fact that the bankers paid themselves hefty bonuses after the crisis did rankle with various social groups and the resentment was expressed through public demonstrations. Nearly 40% of the existing customers closed their accounts and the newer customers did not mind shifting their accounts or demanded a reward for sustained relationship.

The income inequalities, which were becoming a noticeable feature of the emerging social strata looked like applying salt to the wound and fueled the resentment further. Surveys showed that a number of people openly gave vent to their feeling and maintained that they had very little faith in their financial service provider. [we the 99%]

The growing use of the Internet, emergence of Google, Apple, Facebook, and Amazon (GAFA), and social media were impacting the way the social and economic activities were being conducted. Advances in the use of computers, development of sophisticated algorithms, and robots are rudely shaking up the manual work practices in banking and insurance industries. The technological advances drastically modified the banking needs and the ways to meet them. Retaining the customers was becoming difficult against the onslaught of Financial Technologies (FinTech), and disruption by new competitors who were invading the FIs' turf. We would, in the next chapter, describe the FinTech attacks and its impact on eroding the FIs customer base. Briefly put, the FinTechs were attacking the soft underbelly. FIs had to bear a heavy cost burden in complying with the regulatory requirements. The FinTechs had no such need as they did not have regulatory oversight. It would be useful to briefly touch on the competition which FIs have been facing. Unlike in the past the competitors were no longer other FIs but tech savvy companies with a large customer base, very deep pockets, and highly innovative technical expertise. In the USA these could easily be identified as GAFA. In China, we have Alibaba and Ten Cents. They could undertake not only transfer of funds and payments but also lend moneys to customers. These conclusions were arrived at after extensive discussions with bankers, consultants, and those connected with the industry. It became clear that the products offered by the banks could easily be unbundled and the competitors could do cherry picking and "disrupt" the profitable segment. We could briefly draw the following conclusions.

1. Innovations in Financial Services are deliberate and in the short run somewhat predictable
2. The innovations have greatest impact where they employ business models that are platform based, data intensive, and capital light
3. The major impact would be felt in Banking and Insurance
4. The incumbent institutions will employ parallel strategies: aggressively competing with new entrants while leveraging existing assets
5. Collaboration among regulators
6. Such disruptions will not be a one-time affair but would be a continuous pressure to innovate that will shape customer behavior and business models and long-term structure of Financial Services Industry.

It would be seen that the sector is at cross roads. It has certain options. It could take over the FinTechs if possible. The road it takes would depend on where it wants to go. Should the banks close their branches? Should operations be fully digital? In case it was decided to have some branches how should they be manned? Should branches be replaced by Apple stores like entities? Still more complex issues pertain to the transition phase. How do we bring about these changes? Managing the transition is by no means going to be easy.

It would be useful to clarify the way in which we would examine these issues. We would be looking at them from the point of view of a corporate planner. A corporate planner looks at the years gone by and ahead, for the next few years, covering the plan period. Such an approach has two advantages. Firstly, it is firmly rooted in the broad organizational context. Secondly, the balance sheet implications of such proposals have to be kept in mind.

At the moment there is a great uncertainty about the future. The speed with which changes are coming could well be described as hectic. One could make guesses about what the industry is likely to face but the skill lies in anticipating when it would happen. A planner has to take the plunge. The old stars have died, but no new ones are seen.

Many of the macro assumptions which one could take for granted prior to 2016 cannot be considered valid. Deregulation, liberalization, and globalization were the basis for policies pursued for over the past thirty years. They were discarded by many governments. As if this were not enough, the Financial Services Industry had to cope up with political and economic changes arising from the emergence of the so-called nationalist policies. Such policies are today being followed by the USA, UK, and to some extent Austria, Italy, and so on. Even in countries like France and Germany, advocates of such policies seem to be emerging stronger and are trying to bring in such nationalist policies to the extent possible. It is always difficult to summarize the diverse currents that engulf the industry. We have therefore taken recourse to a somewhat archaic method and used the "Oracle of Delphi" technique. Such studies comprising surveys of CEO opinions and views of consultants and leading accountancy firms like PricewaterhouseCoopers (PwC), KPMG, and Ernst & Young (EY) highlight the important currents shaping the socio-economic environment. One could then draw some useful conclusions for one's organization based on the areas of strength and weaknesses.

This book examines all these and tries to generalize about the ones which could affect the industry both in the short run and in the long run. These are not mere academic exercises. One has to take decisions, commit resources, and chart out a course of action. At the same time, one would have to be nimble and be ready to modify/change a chosen course of action. Further the policy options and required responses can be diametrically opposite because the policies implemented by various countries and their governments can be as diverse as can be. We could best illustrate the point by referring to the regulatory scene. The costs for regulatory compliance are ballooning. They would assume considerable importance for the profit and loss account. The real impact is on the operations and the way the business carries out its activities. But currently in the USA the emphasis is on dismantling the regulatory and supervisory apparatus. In the UK supervisors are insisting on stringent regulations. Sam Woods, Deputy Governor and Chief Officer, Prudential Regulation Authority, in his speech at the Mansion House, stated that whatever the future shape of things to come the financial system must be robustly regulated.

The attempt is to see how these problems are met and the difficulties are overcome. Customer needs are no longer the same as in the past and considerable changes have to be made to satisfy them. In the first three chapters we consider the challenges that are coming up and later examine which route the Financial Services sector would take [or has followed] to meet these challenges to bring about a harmonious and symbiotic relationship between the staff and the new Artificial Intelligence (AI) driven performers, like robots. The FIs are going to be called on to serve previously excluded segments from the banks' customer base. In a sense, countries like Kenya and Sub-Saharan countries have shown how even, or perhaps because of a weak financial structure, FinTechs have replaced the banks and have made a significant dent on their profit-making segments.

Various scenarios have and can come up. One such scenario could be a merger of FinTech companies and the existing FIs. The FinTechs are agile, innovative, and not burdened by legacy systems. The FIs have capital resources and a captive customer base to couple these activities and to serve the customers. The customer profile is changing. The customer is not only tech savvy but also wants services 24/7 and from any place. Bankers have to see that they can meet these ever-present challenges thrown up by their competitors.

We would at this stage consider two problems which the FIs had to deal with immediately after they had come out of the crisis. In the immediate aftermath of the crisis, and till about 2016[prior to the Trump era] they had to meet the myriad regulatory requirements that had been imposed. Coupled with the fact that they would be subjected to stress tests was an arduous requirement. In the uncertain world in which FIs operate, this was an extremely difficult imposition. Secondly, the FIs had to prove that they did take their responsibility as trustees and custodians very seriously and that utmost care had to be taken for safeguarding the resources entrusted to their care. Deposit insurance is a mere token and is not a substitute for what that trust could achieve.

Even though this was something within the control of the management, it required a clear examination of their own weaknesses and policy drawbacks. It could also highlight the performance, management policies for rewards and bonuses! There was a public outcry against the bonuses paid particularly since it was clear that the FIs were surviving because of the taxpayers' funds that were made available for rescuing them.

We have made a bare bone analysis of the then prevailing situation because very few management teams show the courage to own their mistakes and to take remedial steps. We have experienced such situations and it is only then that men and boys get separated. Practices which have been in existence for 10 or 15 years have to be changed or at times altogether discarded. This poses immense challenges for the management. Here we must point out to loan foreclosures which some FIs had to undertake [inevitable no doubt]. But it seriously dented reputation and stigmatized the lender institutions. To get back the confidence of the wider affected groups is no mean task.

The period under review was indeed tumultuous. A few well-known institutions failed. Others were groaning under heavy debt burdens. Some others were experiencing the pangs of mergers forced on them. Building capital through investors whose names could help in building confidence meant allotting either preference shares or giving them a sufficiently large chunk of shares and perhaps a board seat too!

We now turn to socio-economic environment which was also undergoing changes. The Financial Services Industry had come to assume that the policy of globalization, liberalization, and deregulation had come to stay and that it was more or less considered inviolable. These assumptions were being challenged and it would not be wrong to say that populist policies like "America First" or "Brexit" were catching the public imagination. These were not mere election slogans but, in many countries, including USA, policies like imposition of tariffs, break up of trade treaties, or even exiting from Paris Climate Agreement became a reality. Coupled with the relaxation of many environmental regulations the socio-economic ethos was radically different from the one in which FIs had been operating for over three decades.

Making forecasts about what lies in the future is a particularly difficult task. But since we are viewing these changes from the perspective of a corporate planner, we look for policy changes that are imminent and have to be taken note of. The global supply chain-based production could come under severe strain. Centers like London which had attained the status of being the World's Financial Capital suddenly lost its primacy and one is left wondering whether leading FIs like Morgan Stanley would shift their European base from London to say, Frankfurt. Equally worrying would be the way World Trade Organization (WTO) would function in the coming era. Similarly, immigration policies are becoming a bone of contention and a cause for major political upheavals. Surveys of CEO opinions, forecasts made by leading consultancy firms, or accountancy organizations become our guides. We present a brief summary of such work done and must say that such conclusions will have to be tailored in the light of other details gathered by the organizations. The official reports of meetings at Basle, speeches delivered by Central Bankers, heads of leading FIs also do provide important guidance notes.

We have in the following pages attempted to highlight the major emerging trends. We must particularly add that in the next chapter we will be considering the disruptive technology developments separately as the impact of FinTech developments warrant a much fuller and elaborate evaluation.

Socio-Economic Factors

We now look at the important socio-economic factors likely to impinge on the working of the institutions. The financial services sector has seen what could well be described as a radical change in the operating environment. The policies pursued in the immediate past, changing profile of the customers, the compliance requirements along with the developments in major political, economic, and technology fields largely determine the future of the financial services sector. These changes significantly affect the functioningF of the FIs.

The speed of change is extremely fast paced and the impact of various factors is picking up and not slowing down. The tasks before the management are humongous. The main difficulty in such an exercise is in anticipating when a given change would take place. One can guess as to the possibility but the problem lies in anticipating when it would happen. Merely to take a look at the major changes in the technical, economic, and political environment and then to guess as to what the future holds was not enough. There is at the moment a great uncertainty about the likely shape of events. Many of the macro assumptions which one could take for granted prior to 2016 could not be considered valid. Who would have thought that USA would withdraw from the Paris Climate Agreement and try and follow an isolationist policy or that the UK would try to be out of the European Union (EU) and severe its relationship with the EU? To be realistic about the likely scenario we must admit that there is no pole star seen to guide our course. One has to move on with heightened uncertainty dogging one's footsteps. Banks, insurance companies, accounting firms, and consultants are intently gazing at the picture and trying to fathom the consequential, emerging problems. These are not mere academic exercises. One has to take decisions, commit resources, and chart out a course of action. At the same time, one would have to try and to arrive at some guiding principles that would be useful for the next two to three years. One would have to be nimble and to modify as one goes along. Obviously, the views and conclusions reached are as diverse as diverse can be. We would point out just one such area and show how difficult it would be to make adjustments. Further, during the last few years all of us in the Financial Services Industry had come to accept Globalization, Deregulation, and Liberalization as the broad parameters of policy. It is no longer so. Additionally, as we would show in the next chapter the technology innovations are taking place at breathtaking pace. New players with very deep pockets (allegedly Apple has idle cash amounting to US $250 Billion) are now straddling the turf. Amazon, as has been reported, is keen on entering banking and is already lending money to small and medium sized enterprises. We are, no doubt, currently witnessing a paradigm shift. Therefore, we have no option but to paint with a broad brush and come out with tentative and a somewhat hazy picture. It is like aiming at a bird which is moving in a zigzag manner and at varying speeds. Before we proceed further, we would summarize briefly the observations of the Secretary General of the United Nations about the impact of the various developments during 2017 and 2018.If one looks at the politics and geopolitical tensions, with the global economy and the megatrends, the truth is that they are more and more interlinked, interfering with each other.

No doubt the global economy is growing at a rate of 3.1% but there are enough indications to suggest that there could be a slowdown. There are risks and only a very healthy global cooperation could help the revival.

The first risk arises on account of imposition of tariffs. The second risk is related to debt that is much higher than in the last financial crisis. It limits the capacity to respond to any potential crisis. Further the capacity to implement the projects to achieve sustainable development goals is hampered. Then we have instability in the financial markets. The Brexit saga shows that if one looks at the problems that have come up, the political system does not know what to do when dealing with problems that have strong economic impacts. Lack of confidence leads to instability in the market.

There is a risk of climate change. We are losing this race. Climate change is running faster than we are. The political will is slowing down in the USA and a few other countries. We see lot of subsidies to fossil fuel being taken away and even carbon pricing being withdrawn. Some are even doubting if the climate change is real! Inequality has increased. Further growth is uneven.

One could go on adding to the list. But the broad conclusions are alarming, and frightening even to a casual reader. For a planner they are as bad as bad can be, and uncertainty is writ large about the possible outcomes.

We had referred CEO surveys, conjectures hinted at by leading consultants, leading accountancy firms operating internationally. We must refer to an ominous warning issued to the author by some CEOs. They have a feeling that the advisers could change their views. But for them such a change can come with a very high cost. Against the background of the serious concerns mentioned by the Secretary General of the United Nations one would expect to be agile and watchful and to examine which particular factors and or segments of the business could be affected (adversely or otherwise). It would be pertinent to briefly review the specific elements of the broader picture painted above and undertake periodic reviews to see how they affect the financial system and the wider economy. The only factor which should be uppermost in the management thinking would be those going drastically against the earlier globalization approaches.

Nationalism vs. Globalization

The Protectionist Policies as embodied in slogans like "America First" have a sway over the public mind and coupled with promises for restoring lost jobs in "reopened coalmines" or "Steel Mills at Pittsburgh" are considered as landmark achievements. Add to this a reversal of the somewhat liberal immigration policies, and one can well imagine how countries like China, India, Israel etc. would worry about their Information Technology (IT) and Export Sectors.

The situation is in an extremely fluid state. It would be difficult to come to firm conclusions regarding the impact of such policy changes on finance and Financial Institutions. We quote the observations of the London Economist of 19th January 2019.

> Recently, though, the character and tempo of globalization have changed. The pace of economic integration around the world has slowed by—though not all-measures. Slow-balization, a term used since 2015 by Adjiedj Bakas, a Dutch trend watcher, describes the reaction against globalization. How severe will it become? How much will a trade war exacerbate? What would global commerce look like? These are questions to which we do not have firm answers. One would have to watch and wait to see how the situation develops. One thing is certain that the reversal of policies would not augur well for the global economy.

We would have to have a halfway house to a disaster scenario and somewhat hesitant adjustment.

Regulation vs. Deregulation

The crisis of 2007–2009 showed the recklessness, no doubt driven by greed, with which FIs behaved. They could be saved only by tax payers' money and the same institutions are now wanting to have total freedom from the yoke of regulatory measures. On the other hand, countries having huge debt burdens (non-performing assets) and other problems would like stiff regulation.

Demographic Changes

Apart from the absolute numbers, the demographic composition shows a major shift in the composition. In fact, it is significant from an operational point of view. The proportion of the elderly is increasing and at the same time the Governments do not seem to be keen on sharing this burden of looking after them since their budgets are groaning under the burden of such social costs. The absorption of refugees from war torn countries like Syria by Western European countries, are straining the social security net in these countries at the seams. The insurance industry should examine the changes and come out with suitable policies and pension schemes. It could be a lucrative segment which could boost their shrinking profits!

Further the financial management needs of these groups are different and their approach to technology is also distinctly different. The younger set is keen on mobile and digital technology and perhaps is not keen on branch visits. The elderly would like to visit and meet the concerned staff in person. It is doubtful if they would be satisfied with a robot answering their queries. According to them in all probability, investment propositions can be suitably examined only at branches or offices of their brokers.

Lack of Trust in FIs

The disappearance of personal bond which the customers had with their Bankers/Brokers/Insurance Agents is slowly getting eroded. The kind of relationship which the elderly had with the managers/staff is slowly diluted to the extent that today the managers would hardly recognize very few of their clients. A large number of customers hardly visit their branches and have no need for a brick and mortar model of banking or brokering. They prefer to be on their own and would take decisions without a banker/ broker coming in! We must add here that during discussions on the feasibility of fully digital branches "manned" by robot advisers did not find favor with a large number of seniors present.

We must look at this aspect in depth to assess how "trust" becomes a key component of the social capital that enables participants to act together more effectively to pursue mutually beneficial objectives. It is to some extent true that inequality could be regarded as an important reason for decline in trust. It could render some economic policies less fair or drive a wedge between socio-economic groups. However, in this case the most important factor is the FI's own behavior.

In fact, during the last two decades one remembers the bankruptcy of some leading players (Lehman Brothers) or the rescue by the World Bank/ IMF or the Central Banks which regulated these institutions. There is perhaps exasperation when one notices that one of the important factors for the debacle is nothing else but greed. Even at the cost of repetition we would say that the banks and FIs must remember that long lasting trust relationship will not be created through "TRUST PROJECTS". A set of clearly articulated and continually reinforced values and principles which are strictly adhered to would have to be the foundation stone on which customer centric culture is set and followed by the staff at all levels. No wonder Dr. Mervyn King (Governor [Retired] of Bank of England) has chosen a somewhat shocking title for his book "*End of Alchemy—Money, Banking and the Future of the Global Economy*." These are not mere anguished expressions but are rooted in customer surveys. Nearly 40% of the banks' customers have moved away or reduced their dependence on their banks as their primary service providers for financial services and another 20% have plans to shift away. Trust influences economic activity. It reduces transaction costs (Insurance and Legal etc.).

Trust promotes cooperation and reduces recourse to collective action to resolve problems. The regaining of trust is indeed quite a mammoth task. It will have to be a strong value premise for most of the actions vis-a-vis the customers never to be lost sight of. It must become a part of total commitment and not a once and all ritual to be performed. No doubt, there are other equally important problems facing the organizations. These also present challenges for the management of unprecedented magnitude. To tackle these, great efforts are indeed needed. These would, in addition, would strain financial resources no end.

Concerns Among Staff Members

At the ground level there are considerable anxieties for the staff about the possibility of having continued employment with the banks or insurance companies. Many routine and comparatively low skilled jobs are already being taken over by machines and there is every possibility that even small loan processing (mortgages, automobiles) lending and risk analysis would soon be undertaken by machines. One would have in the near future to worry about machines and robots replacing the humans. It must be mentioned that several algorithms are commercialized and are operational. Many of these are developed in-house using newer computer languages and are proprietary to a given bank or FI. Banks and FIs may have to deal with a very peculiar problem. On the one hand they may have to reduce some of their existing staff while they would have to reckon with difficulties in recruiting highly trained staff to undertake data analysis, or deal with and develop AI-based programs. [Refer Chap. 10 on Human Resources Management]

We have already touched on the emergence of new players, like GAFA, in Financial Services Sector. We now deal at some length with the review of other equally important problems referred to in the reports mentioned earlier. Given below is a list of some of these:

- Concern over data protection particularly in the areas where the FIs are likely to be affected
- Transparency in asset and wealth management activities
- Likely slowdown in economic growth
- Cyber-Security
- Cloud Computing
- Payments Confusion
- New Competitive Threats
- Decentralization of Digital Infrastructure

We have extracted these from various sources and it goes to show how diverse the problem areas are.

In a globalized environment manufacturing sector has trans-national supply chains and assembly units. These were located in various South-East Asian countries due to cost considerations. Today the major concern is about the supply chain disruption.

In a survey undertaken by Deloitte in 2018, 50% of the respondents felt that Financial Services would change significantly and more particularly in Asia and in the Pacific region. 68% of the Capital Market Firms expect major changes. They are equally certain that the insurance sector would also undergo major changes. Some other reports highlighted changing customer expectations and their determinants. There are apprehensions that harnessing technological change is perhaps detrimental . AI being included in command and control centers is sending shudders down the spine of many observers. There are others who worry about highly skilled jobs lying vacant. How could small companies ever expect to get data analysts etc.? Their salaries are already very high and are increasing by 16% every year.

At a ground level, competition from nontraditional players with skills, funding, and attitude could be a major factor to be reckoned with. They are of the firm view that cost containment and search for revenue opportunities would be a major source for top line growth for FIs. A strong plea is made for having a long-term perspective. In a decade, market leaders would help in financing infrastructure, enabling commerce, preserve and expand wealth and help consumers lead a better life. The idea is that the needs would not go away, though the ways through which these are fulfilled could undergo a change. The leading banks and insurance companies would have to show the way ahead by making difficult choices and focusing on capabilities that set them apart from their peers, and saying NO to that which is not essential. They would guide others in how best technology could be harnessed to serve existing and future clients. They could point to others how effective partnering with innovators and experimenting with new business models.

It seems certain that AI, Machine Learning (ML), and Robotics would take over many of these functions. The problem is to see that these are enmeshed with the existing systems. The coping decisions will have to be made. These could be innumerable and would be a severe drain on resources.

We would briefly say that the journey ahead is going to be extremely difficult. The new players, freed from the regulations and legacy systems, are already undercutting traditional niche businesses. The FIs have taken steps to meet capital adequacy norms but they have not succeeded in getting the economics of business right. An in-house development or acquisitions may point to certain direction. Further newer "hair-cut equity" may become the new Mantra for raising capital. Some of the aspects touched on in this chapter would be considered in some detail in the subsequent two chapters.

Over the last several years, we have been associated with bringing about such changes and found that the various management persons associated with this work would benefit largely if some of the suggestions listed below were to be followed. These are summarized below as a rough guide for those initiating such changes.

1. Establishing a sense of urgency
2. Forming a powerful guiding coalition
3. Creating a vision
4. Communicating the vision
5. Empowering others to act on the vision
6. Planning for creating short-term wins
7. Consolidating improvements and producing more change
8. Institutionalizing new approaches.

Sometimes urgency leads to elimination of intermediate steps. Many intermediate phases that the change process goes through require considerable time. Predetermined deadlines are arbitrary and could harm the ultimate results. Skipping steps creates an illusion of speed but satisfactory results may not follow. Critical mistakes at a late stage in development can have devastating effects. This does not mean that there should be no sense of urgency.

It should be highlighted that in this transformation process decisions would be required over a wide range of issues. More particularly emphasis would be on development of cognitive skills. And these will have to be sharpened. The decisions will have to be on the fly. Customers would not wait till you complete your formalities in your decision making. We would, in the next Chapter, discuss the way FIs could respond to the "Disruption" threat. There would be specific problems and these need to be resolved quite differently.

We conclude on the note that the Financial Services Industry is in ferment as never before and we are perhaps likely to be witness to a radical shift in business priorities that would entail a change in the underlying business model.

CHAPTER 2

Technology Challenges: Impact Assessment

In the post 2008 to 2010 crisis period, a major factor impinging on the FIS' working was the technology factor. There were significant developments on the IT front. It is therefore absolutely essential to review these changes and to assess their impact. It should, however, be pointed out that the first three chapters are interconnected and that it is only for analytical convenience that they have been segregated.

At the outset, it would be useful to point out that the book keeping and work systems of Financial Institutions have a dual purpose. Basically, it is to ensure trust in contracts. Many documents also embody settled legal decisions. In a sense, technological innovations are intertwined with finance. Today's system is the product of fifteenth century accounting system and the ledgers too served the building of trust. The telegraph in 1860 and the typewriters have created the plumbing of modern payments, clearing, and settlement infrastructure required by the global financial settlement systems. Now we have ATMs, online banking, and since 1980, the mobile.

The post crisis period witnessed major disruptions to the bank's business model. FinTech's true promise springs from its potential to unbundle FIs products into its core functions of payment, settlement, maturity transformations, sharing of risks, and allocation of capital. This possibility is taken advantage of by the new entrants. They are the new payment service providers, aggregators, peer-to-peer lenders, and providers of innovative trading platforms.

V. C. Joshi, *Digital Finance, Bits and Bytes*,
https://doi.org/10.1007/978-981-15-3431-7_2

At this stage, it would be useful to have a critical look at what disruption really means. The theory of disruptive innovation, was published by M. Christensen in his article in Harvard Business Review of December 2015 issue—"Disruption describes a process where by a smaller company with fewer resources is successfully able to challenge an established incumbent business." In the eight-year period under review, there were more than 450 institutions trying to grab portions of FI business. The areas covered new digital currencies, wallets, and so on. It must also be said that fewer than five of these survived as stand-alone entities.

The established bigger units respond to these challenges in various ways. These units try to bring about qualitative changes in the product or its' pricing. There are at times neglected elements which are targeted by smaller units and the bigger units could start paying attention to them. At the same time, the incumbents could try and move up market and use the advantages achieved in their early success. The trouble starts when the main stream customers start adopting newer entrant's offerings and then voluminous disruption occurs. A de-segregation of the FIs balance sheet shows that 59% of earnings flow from pure fee products. The loan segment, because of provision requirements, shows a return on these products of only 20% to 25%. It is no wonder that the disruptors exploit these payments and fee earning products.

Additionally, the Financial Services sector adopted an equally significant approach to meet these challenges. There was a need for the FIs to reduce the costs generally and particularly for "thin-file" customers. The idea was to have a hard look at the business model and to see if the reduced costs would make the "thin-file" customers a viable proposition. To pursue "inclusive" banking policies FIs brought in truly innovative practices like digital credit scoring and lending to be obtained through the use of mobile phones or social media interactions.

The smaller units had considerable need for the capital to grow. It was logical for the FIs to supply the same and to use their captive customer base. It was natural that banks and FIs just took over the smaller companies. Figure 2.1 shows how advantageous it would be for banks and FinTechs to join hands and work together (preferable option—merger).

But the picture was complicated when the challenges emanated from companies like Amazon, Alibaba, or Apple. They had deep pockets, a large customer base, and most important of all idle cash. At one time, Apple had parked huge cash deposits in Ireland. The threats these companies pose through their attempts at taking over some of the disaggregated functions

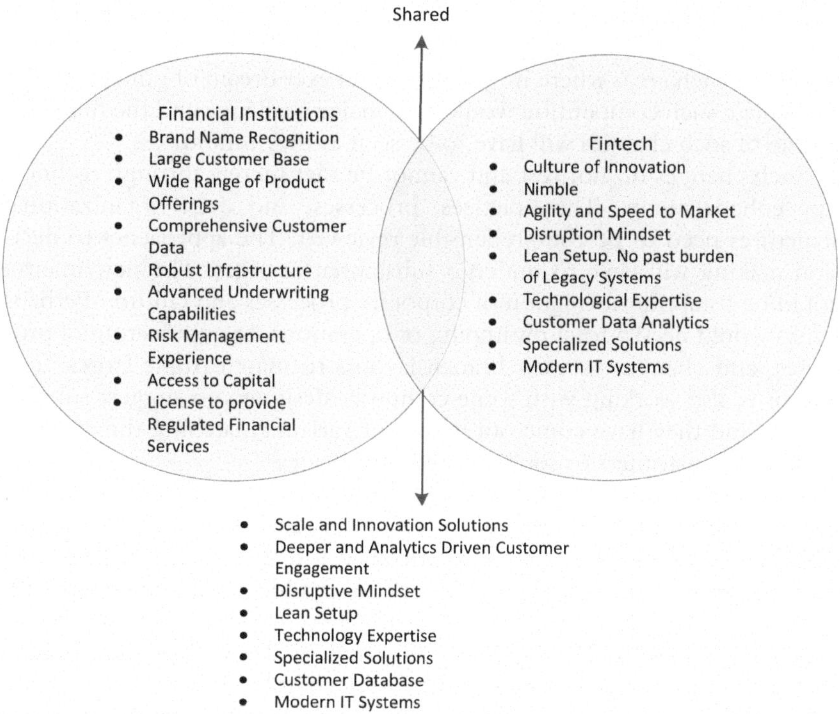

Fig. 2.1 Advantages and disadvantage of collaborations/mergers. (Source: World Economic Forum)

looms large forever. In fact, they have already taken over large portions of money transfers or lending money for shorter periods to SMEs and undertake micro loaning. Amazon's extending supplier credit for a period of six months to a year has already made dents in what could be described as trade finance.

It is necessary also to bear in mind that the strategic context undergoes a change when a given technology gains momentum. The structure of competition, conduct of business, and ultimately even relations among the industries do and could change. To stay ahead of the unfolding trends, FIs would need to be constantly reviewing the field and be nimble to change the strategy. Just to give one example we could show how threatening such emerging challenges can be. Singapore Post with its vast network, its logistic and warehousing backbone, would be entering the E-commerce field. In India, the post office has already entered the banking field and the postmen reach areas where no banker would ever dream of going. For FIs to manage such competition would be a major challenge and the full magnitude of such changes will have to be seen as they unfold.

Such changes do not rest and cannot be met merely through technology enhancements. The practices, processes, and even organizational structures need to be comprehensibly reviewed. The approaches to decision making will have to undergo substantial changes. The new mantra could be total transformation of corporate processes and culture. Perhaps banks would need a total revamping of operations, re-engineering of processes, and changes to their branch layouts to match Apple stores. The author is also working with some computer designers to suggest suitable layouts and they have come out with four variants matching the needs of small rural customers to sophisticated urban ones.

Further, pressures on technology transformations emanate from customer expectations. The millennial customers and their succeeding generations want a "quick and sensibly priced customer service". Such services have to be available anywhere, anytime, and additionally equipped with facilities for transferring from one channel to another. The day to day transactions have to be effortless and seamless. They want their branch visits to be rare and only for something important like problem resolution. The problems have to be such as could not be resolved otherwise. Some of the customers have told us that it should be possible for them to switch from one entity to another.

At this stage, we would briefly touch on a survey conducted by Ernst and Young for the British Banks Association. It highlights the fact that there are about 180 mobile clicks per second by the customers for executing their banking transactions. Mobile banking has unbelievably changed the way we meet our banking requirements. Table 2.1 briefly reviews how

Table 2.1 Devices used in financial transactions

Customer	*Desktops (%)*	*Smart phones (%)*	*Tablets (%)*
Young generation	33	60	6
Millennials	38	47	11
GenX	41	45	11
Elderly	47	46	6

other devices apart from mobile phones are currently deployed in financial transactions.

The Financial Stability Board in its report of 2017 points out a number of potential benefits and risks as listed below, for financial stability arising out of technology adoptions and consequential disruptions.

- The more efficient processing of information in credit decisions, reviewing financial markets, and critical evaluation of insurance contracts should contribute to the creation of an efficient financial system.
- Artificial Intelligence (AI) and Machine Learning (ML) would help regulators in ensuring compliance and increased supervisory effectiveness.
- Lack of interoperability or auditability of AI and ML could become a macro level risk for data security and adherence to protocols.
- Adequate testing and training users for ensuring that applications do what they are expected to.

In the face of daunting challenges facing financial services industry, one would have thought that FIs would be trying very hard to build up sinews and fibers to meet the challenges ahead. We must say that while the problems are well appreciated, the industry seems to have taken only a few symbolic steps. These include creation of innovation centers, centers for excellence, or having sand boxes. But a more detailed, rugged preparedness is what is required. The steps taken by various organizations do not quite reflect that they are well prepared to meet the challenges ahead. Table 2.2 brings out what is stated above.

Table 2.2 Regional preparedness

Regions	*Fully prepared (%)*	*Considered important (%)*
USA	7	23
Europe	6	40
Asia Pacific	14	61
Emerging markets	18	62

Source: Compiled by author

It is true that implementing such decisions would involve substantial expenditure on the part of FIs. Some of them are perhaps not in a position to do so. A brief analysis shows that the following could account for such behavior on part of FIs:

- Shrinking margins
- Underutilization of assets
- Non-availability of skilled manpower
- Lack of revenue growth/flat earnings
- Burden of non-performing assets

We have in the previous sections, repeatedly adduced to the fact that massive reorganization on many fronts would be essential. The effort is not restricted to creating a small department or unit or asking an existing IT section to take over. These are essentially top management level decisions and a total commitment for implementation at the CEO and other senior management personnel.

We had in Chap. 1 referred to consultants and accounting firms making forecasts about the changing scenarios. The same firms have made predictions about possible technology scenarios. Some of these firms have even gone to the extent of suggesting revamping of boards of directors and also in shifting the focus from return on investment to a much wider front. They even recommend induction of technology experts on the boards to guide the senior management (a tall order indeed). However, like time and tide, changes do not wait for organizations to make decisions on technology matters. Suffice it to say that during the years 2014 to 2016, numerous algorithms for use in financial services were developed and were ready for use. Technology implementations have to be on the same level as earlier slogans like "export or die".

Technology Trends

We have deliberately avoided the use of the term "revolutionary" to describe these changes. We must appreciate that the core functions are still being performed by the humans but undertaking major restructuring required for technology changes to be fully and properly put to use is not taking place. The reason is lack of skilled manpower to handle sophisticated computerized processes. One must be aware however that restructuring is indeed called for and we would deal with these aspects in Chap.

10 on Human Resources how lower skilled jobs would soon be handled by machines.

Against this background, we now review the changes that are taking place on the technology front. It would be obvious to anyone that the financial services industry has one great asset which would be the envy of all its competitors (leaving aside Facebook, Google, and others). It is not surprising that this data bank has come to be known as "Big Data". Very often there is a criticism that big is not quantified. We do not subscribe to this view. For the sake of argument, let us look at the definition of the word "Wind". Wind is defined as movement of air, but how much air or speed at which it should move are not mentioned. Do these omissions affect our understanding of Wind?

We, however, do appreciate attempts at bringing about certain precision and turn to a paper aptly titled "Undefined by data—Big Data Definitions" by Jonathan Stuart Ward. The term is widely used not merely by academics and industry but by media, consultants, and marketing people. The tech companies have tried to define it by looking at the characteristics. Gartner defines it by referring to volume, variety, and velocity. Oracle, on the other hand states that big data is the derivation of value from business data, augmented with new structured data. On the other hand, Intel defines it with reference to data created. It is linked to an organization which generates a median 300 Terabytes weekly. Microsoft in its definition links it to serious computing power used in machine learning, an often highly complex set of information.

It is obvious that these attempts are not fully satisfactory. We however start with the argument that most readers are aware as to what we are referring to. Any further quibbling and hair splitting would not throw greater light on this. We are suggesting a very crude measuring rod. The data analysis team should feel convinced that their requirements for deducing inferences are met and that analysts are convinced that what they are dealing with is big data.

Prof. Nate Silver in his renowned work titled "Signal and Noise" has a very illuminating comment on the subject—"Sheer numbers have no way of speaking for themselves. We speak for them. We ascribe meaning to them in self-serving ways that are detached from their objective reality." The failure of risk models in prediction of the crisis shows how fragile such models are—part of the problem is we try to find meaning where none exists.

If the quantity of information is increasing by 2.5 quintillion, the amount of knowledge is certainly not increasing. There may be many hypotheses to test, many data sets to mine, but a relatively constant amount of truth. We can never make perfectly objective predictions; the subjective biases can never be removed.

It is against this, that we should look at Big Data technology and what it refers to. Basically, the following four aspects are covered in usage.

- Data Storage
- Data Processing arrangement
- Data Management
- Data Analytics

Data Analysis comprises:

- Query and reporting
- Data visualization
- Predictive modeling
- Optimization
- Simulation
- Geo spatial analysis
- Natural language test and voice analysis.

It would be pertinent to issue a general warning regarding the conclusions that are drawn. We must accept a certain degree of uncertainty and probability. As planners, we would like the organizations to learn to accept these two elements in the predictions we tend to make.

We now turn to review the data collected by Financial Institutions. The sources for getting data are varied. Directed data is obtained from the direct gaze of surveillance technology on a place or person. Automated data is obtained from human activities on digital devices, global positioning systems, and photographs. Volunteered data is acquired from individuals who willingly give their information, sometimes through a common system used by a large number of people on social media.

The data could be structured or unstructured. Much of the data is obviously created in real time. After all we need to ensure timeliness of access to data, data granularity and variety. At this stage, we would turn to another question that is frequently raised at seminars or at training sessions. Most of the participants are intrigued by the question as to where exactly does such data gets stored. What happens to the data stored in Cloud?

This data is stored at centers that are built in abandoned mines, beneath the mountains, and even in underground caverns. Bunkers are becoming prime spaces for retrofitting data centers. Bunkering data in disaster proof subterranean centers designed to withstand category 5 hurricanes, electromagnetic pulses, and long-lasting storms are becoming increasingly common. Some organizations require their data to be triple replicated and distributed in geographically dispersed facilities.

The consumer protection authority in the UK has suggested certain agreements between the facility providers and their clients. Care has to be taken to ensure that certain rights which the clients have (when your storage facility is shifted), the client needs to know in advance. Cases of hacking have also come to light and the agreement should be very specific about the responsibilities of the parties concerned.

Big Data Analytics

Big Data Analytics is a process of examining huge amounts of data. Some authors categorize it to include even collection, organizing, and critically analyzing these vast quantities of data. Basically, there are two types—stream processing and batch processing. In stream processing, the data as the name suggests, comes in streams and is processed as soon as possible in real time. Storm and Apache Kafka are popular stream processing models. In batch processing, however, the data is collected and processed/analyzed at a later time as needed. Figure 2.2 shows how the data flows during the analytical processing. At a lecture in Bangalore in December 2016, the author was stopped and asked to explain the connotation of term "orthogonal" data sets. These sets are unstructured and could be even in the form of free text.

Generally, a well-defined system is based on four core attributes.

- Talent—availability plus pipeline
- Capital—Seed Capital, Growth Capital, and Listed Capital
- Policy—Regulatory Regimes, Government Programs, Taxation Policies
- Demand—Consumer Demand, Corporate Demand, Demand from other FIs

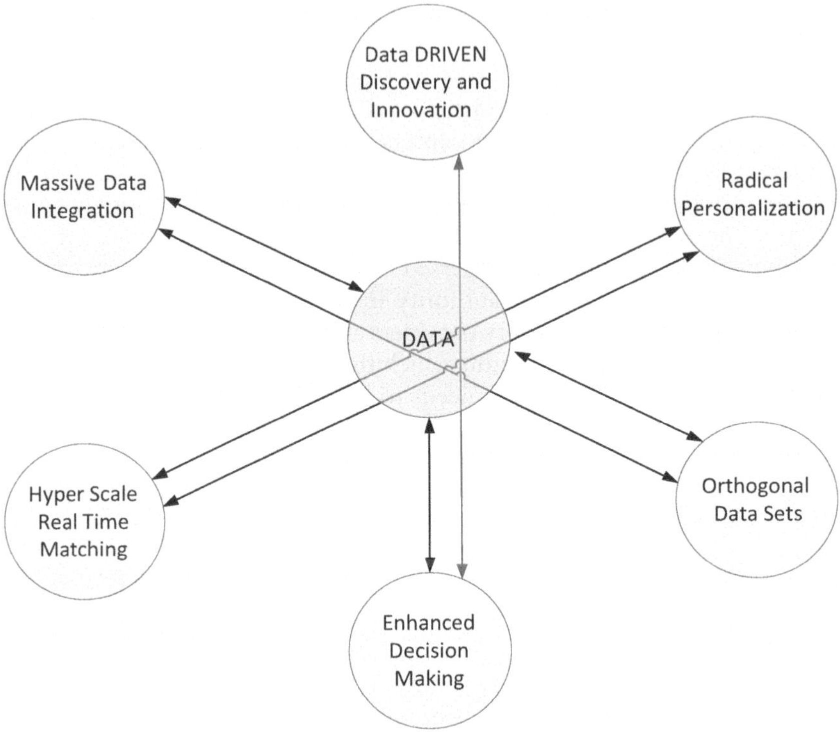

Fig. 2.2 Data flow in analytical process. (Source: The age of analytics: Competing in a data-driven world. A new report from the McKinsey Global Institute (MGI). https://www.mckinsey.com/~/media/McKinsey/Business%20Functions/McKinsey%20Analytics/Our%20Insights/The%20age%20of%20analytics%20Competing%20in%20a%20data%20driven%20world/MGI-The-Age-of-Analytics-Executive-summary.ashx)

It must be stated that this data, apart from being used internally, can be sold. In view of privacy rules, great care needs to be taken in undertaking such transactions.

We now detail the areas where results from analysis could be of assistance to the users in the organization.

- Customer Focused: Credit Scoring, Uses of Banks Products and Schemes like mortgages, consumer credits, alerts for the clients, and new schemes/products arising from specific problems like fluctuations in client's income.

- Operations Focused: Risk Management, Market Impact Analysis
- Regulatory Compliance: Particular attention to Privacy Protection and laws relating to it.
- Training and Portfolio Management

Big Data Implementation: Review of Best Practices

The earlier information systems relied on captured information. The emphasis was on capturing transactions (physical/economic). Big Data now poses a challenge to enterprises of a different kind. It arises from configuration of information pools, past and present, structured and unstructured, formal and informal, social and economic which are constantly evolving in their constant presentation. (Alnoor Bhimani, Journal of Information technology 2015, 30-66/69 doc. 110.1057). Big data adds an analytics dimension to organizational capabilities and unleashes a variety of strategic reorientation.

With the way data flows in strategy, structured information paradigm gets changed. The firm's strategies are to a large extent predicated on technological structures. Information systems are involved in the shifting dynamics of altered information access and use as part of a wider complex loop of intervention and analysis. We are now able to capture customer choices.

At this stage, we must add that great attention will have to be paid to the quality of data. One can't forget that big data comprises many systemic biases. Almost 15% of information obtained is based on Twitter feeds and as such, drawing conclusions from such information has to be done very carefully.

We now shift our attention to problems of adoption. There are four main features which pertain to the training of staff. These are—Educate, Explore, Engage, and Execute.

1. Educate—To succeed, considerable investment would be necessary for training the people. Training will have to be focused on knowledge gathering and market observation.
2. Explore—At higher managerial levels emphasis will have to be on strategy and road map.

3. Engage—Involving staff members in piloting big data initiatives. Only then could they realize the value of the data and appreciate requirements at various levels.
4. Execute—Many a time, the data analysts assume a greater role in deciding on the information collected. During meetings of bankers with faculty members of management institutes and technology consultants far greater attention was paid to the requirements of this group and others played a very passive role. We are of the view that potential outcomes should be very clearly stated by people who are responsible for operational results. Potential Outcomes could be Customer centric, operational, expected risks, new product requirements, employee collaboration (indicative).

In conclusion, we would say that great care needs to be taken in recording, retention, and management of information. Data analysis has to dovetail in the context of business requirement. Implementation is primarily a business decision. We are aware that a considerable amount of interaction will be involved with all concerned.

Many a person have told us that it is always advisable not to be after "Big Bang Solution". The best practice would be to start small, identifying specific high value opportunities. Think Big but Act Small.

The following areas will have to be carefully assessed and decided on.

- Specific Plans for Storage, Retention, Discarding, and Management of data.
- A constant evaluation of data requirements. Perhaps a small group entrusted with this task would be of great use.
- One has to remember that data analysts use different languages. Care therefore has to be taken to see that knowledge is transferred to the concerned staff members.
- The assumptions underlying and the limitations have to be constantly reviewed and examined.
- Previous investment should be properly utilized and not discarded.
- And lastly, a cultural shift to the data-based objective decision making has to be inculcated among the staff members and decision makers.

We must point out to the hurdles which might crop up and prevent the organization from getting the vast benefits of data analysis. Many a time, business goals are not clarified properly. One could be hampered by a shortage of data analysts and operational staff may not quite realize the difficulties in the use of techniques. There are a number of regulations to ensure that data in respect of individual customers is very carefully protected. Important legal issues can come up and strict adherence to such rules is an absolute must.

Cloud Computing

Despite its many forms, Cloud computing services have three distinct characteristics that differentiate them from traditional computing.

1. They are sold on demand, typically by the minute or by the hour.
2. They are demand flexible, in that a user can have as much or as little a service as the user wants.
3. The services and resources are totally managed by the provider. All that the user needs would be personal computer and Internet for connectivity.

A Cloud can be private or public. Vendors in a public cloud can sell it to anyone and it is a shared resource. A private cloud refers to a proprietary network or vendor supplied, hosted services to a well-defined set of users. The goal is to provide easily scalable and secure services.

Recently, F.C.A. (UK) issued a following guidelines for the benefit of users and we give below a very brief summary.

- Customers may (in practice) have a limited scope to tailor the service.
- Provider may move customer data with less visibility and control for the owner.
- Provider may contract out part of the service provided, without the customer's knowledge.

The "Regulated" firms have additionally to worry about the following aspects.

- Legal and regulatory considerations
- Risk Management
- International Standards
- Oversight of service providers

- Data Security and Protection
- Effective Access to Data
- Access to Business premises
- Continuity

Artificial Intelligence and Machine Learning

The contours of Artificial Intelligence (AI) and Machine Learning (ML) are not well defined. But generally, AI refers to machines designed to act intelligently and mimic human decision making whereas Machine Learning refers to the ability of software to learn and self-improve.

Rise of AI in Financial Services

AI is aimed at doing things with the help of technology that are normally done by humans. The National Business Institute survey shows that almost 40% of the respondents confirmed using such technologies like "Predictive Analytics", "Recommendation Engines", "Machines that undertake Voice Recognition and Responses". In a way, these developments are somewhat half-hazard. Only 6% of the organization surveyed had an innovation leader. In fact, AI covers everything from business operations, customer service, marketing, and risk management. All these activities can easily benefit from the applications of AI. Yet, many of the respondents were apprehensive that AI technology was new, untested, and had rather weak security features.

It would not be wrong to assert that wide spread adoption of cognitive systems across a broad range of industries would drive world-wide revenues.

In the Financial Services area, it should be possible to achieve what is envisaged above.

- Explosive Growth in Big Data
- Cheaper Computational Resources
- Smarter Algorithms
- Cloud Computing
- Connected Devices

Continuing progress in AI and ML would be essential to the development of advanced robotics and in knowledge work automation. Mobile

Internet, Internet of Things (IoT), and Cloud Technology are driving developments forcefully. Machines are slowly seeping into our lives. How we live, work, and even entertain are being affected. Voice Powered Assistants like Siri and Alexa are the first sign posts in our journey in this direction. In the final analysis, a true AI system is one that can learn on its own. We are referring to Google's Deep Mind which can make connections and reach meanings without relying on predetermined behavioral algorithms. True AI can improve on past iterations getting smarter and more aware about allowing to enhance itself.

Some of our readers may feel alarmed at these developments. We must say that so called AI developments are a reflection of advanced ML. It is a software with extensive behavioral algorithms that adapt themselves to our likes and dislikes but so far cover only elementary aspects of mechanizing work. No doubt they are useful and are slowly improving their skills. They have however, not reached a level where they are controlling us as if we were "pawns" in their hands.

Coming specifically to Financial Services, we have to take note of some of the factors shaping the developments.

- A new Battle Field for customer loyalty
- Need for Self-Driving Financial Activity
- Future Customer Experiences will be centered on AI which automates customers' financial needs
- Collective Solutions for Shared Activities

AI today promises to solve major problems but a certain degree of danger lurks in the inscrutable black box. Many are worried that it may contain unethical use of data and potential job displacement. Industrial Robots are advancing at a rapid pace. They can improve the speed, quality, and cost of goods and services but they would displace a large number of workers. This possibility challenges a traditional benefits model of tying healthcare and retirement savings to jobs. In an economy that employs workers in a big way, we do need to think about how to deliver benefits to displaced workers. If automation makes jobs less secure, there needs to be a way to deliver benefits outside of employment. Flexicurity or flexible security is one idea for providing health care, education, and housing assistance. It would also cover some way of financing a long-term educational needs and worker retraining. No matter how working life is organized, there need to be ways for people to live fulfilling lives.

Subject to such innovative policies being adopted, there could be much lesser opposition to introducing of AI and ML.

We can't forget that digital banking is the default channel for many customers. There are quite a few who need only channel service provision. We would however add here that an effective combination of human and digital services would be a more appropriate solution. Some European banks have seen changes at a scale where as a result of such combination saw their business growing at the rate of 20% over the last two to three years. Just to hammer home the point made above we would say that today almost 80% of all the customer touch points occur digitally. About 60% of customers use only digital channels. One of the main reasons for increasing use of AI is the impact on costs and consequent savings. The number of branches in Spain and Italy has come down by about 40%. Further existing branches can focus on complex products with remote teams leveraging tools such as video conferencing and screen sharing.

The customer responses vary product-wise and vary from Savings Deposits to Credit Cards and Mortgages. It is very clear that advisory functions are increasingly conducted through digital channels. It would be useful to add that coupled with data analytics, customers can get great value through a bank or FI personalizing service across channels.

For the benefit of readers not closely associated with FSI we show in Table 2.3 how data analysis and AI can be used.

One could easily identify the areas where considerable use of data could be of assistance to the FSI experts. We could easily identify the following two areas.

Table 2.3 Data analysis

Volume • Transaction files • Records • Streams • Sensor data • Social media	*Velocity* • Real time data • Stream computing
Veracity • Unstructured • Uncertainty	*Variety* • Structured • Unstructured • Semi-structured

Source: Author

Customer focus:

- Credit Scoring
- Bank Schemes
- Consumer Credit
- Alerts for Clients
- Devising schemes for cases where there are fluctuations

Operation focus:

- Risk Management
- Market Impact Analysis
- Trading and Portfolio Management
- Regulatory Compliance

We have seen that AI refers to the ability of a computer enabled robotic system to process information and produce outcomes in a manner similar to that of the human thought process. Analytics is a new approach to information discovery and decision making.

A very important and essential activity is meeting the regulatory requirement. For instance, most of the regulators require liquidity planning, and/or asset and liability management. The requirements warrant a rethinking of point in time liquidity positions. These are not sufficient from regulatory point of view. What is required is a real time view.

It would be useful to add that through ML, it would be possible to identify abnormal information.

There are three pillars for such analysis—Product Management, Productization, and Clean Thinking. These three pillars drive the organization toward the vision of delivering client-oriented value by being product centric and market driven. The ability to unlock marketable or income generating insights, it is necessary to evaluate the quality of data. Perhaps a word of caution at this stage is necessary. Big Data analysis contains many systemic biases. As an example, we might see that approximately 15% of the information collected is from Twitter feeds. By analyzing these messages, one cannot say that the analysis holds good for the entire population. We must take care to see that after the analysis we get the following.

- Customer centric outcomes
- Operational Optimization

- New Business Models
- Employee Collaboration

A corporate planner can easily obtain multi-year planning with predictive analysis for stability and capacity, impacts on business through product revenues, volume identification, and cross sale abilities. The ability to unlock marketable income generating insights is absolutely necessary in such analysis.

Augmented and Virtual Reality

Augmented Reality (AR) superimposes computer-generated image(s) on a user's view of the real world thus providing composite picture. Virtual Reality (VR) on the other hand is a computer-generated simulation of a three-dimensional image of an environment that can be interacted with a seemingly real or physical way by a person using a special electronic equipment. It could be a helmet with a screen. It must be understood that VR is an artificial environment that is created with software and presented to the user in such a way that the user suspends beliefs and accepts it as a real environment.

At the core, AR transforms volumes of data and analytics into images or animations that are overlaid on the real world. In practice, most AR applications are delivered through mobile devices. Increasingly delivery will shift to hands free wearables such as head mounted displays, or smart glasses. It would be worth mentioning that AR is supplementing or replacing a number of traditional manuals and training methods at a very fast pace. AR thus enables a new information paradigm which will have a profound impact on how data is structured, managed, and delivered on the Internet. Flat screens have limitations. AR allows people to process the physical and digital simultaneously eliminating the need mentally to bridge the two.

A picture is worth a thousand words. A picture that superimposes information on the physical world reduces the cognitive distance for us. Speed at which information is transmitted and absorbed and the cognitive distance involved in applying it lies at the root of the need for AI. There is no better Graphical User Interface (GUI) than the physical world we see around us. When it is enhanced by a digital overlay of relevant data and guidance where and when they are needed. Many standard instructional methods are quite expensive. AR addresses these issues in real time, on-site, step-by-step visual guidance on various tasks. Further, AR enabled devices can also transmit what an on-site user is seeing to an expert who can see what the worker is seeing and then help him/her. A worker wearing smart glasses would be able to walk a line of factory machines and see their performance parameters. It would then be possible to adjust each and every machine without physically touching it.

It might be useful to compare VR with AR. While AR superimposes digital information on physical world, VR replaces physical reality with a computer-generated environment. VR is useful when settings involved are hazardous or remote. When needed AR can always add a fourth capability viz. simulation to AR's core capabilities to visualize, interact, and instruct.

Combining AR and VR allows users to transcend distance, time, and/or simulate possible future situations. It could even transcend scales by allowing users to engage with environments that are either too small or too big to experiment with directly.

AR creates business value in two ways, first by becoming part of the product themselves and second by improving performance across the value chain. The way products convey important operational and safety information to users can become a point of differentiation. With smart glasses, a user can see an AR display on any product enabled to communicate with them. Perhaps, AR would be of great help in cost reduction.

We are of the view that at the moment there is not much scope for using these technologies either in marketing or in investment advisory services. After all, FI products are intangible and there is no question of "fitting" them in a given environment. However, the industry is trying and as suggested by Bram Nawgin in his paper we find that there are about eight to nine applications for AR and VR in Financial Services Industries.

1. Visualizing "data" is an important tool and helps bond dealers, traders in their day-to-day working. At the same time, it could also be shown to investors for information or in support of decisions made
2. Wealth management software adds certain elements to give users better access to algorithms and trading tools
3. Making payments be made a virtual experience
4. Inclusion of biometric security in VR
5. Helping customers identifying branches or ATMs, mainly during crisis/visits to unknown places
6. Virtual Branch visits
7. Recruitment and Training
8. Demonstrating Bank's use of technology in operation

There are VR tools which enable investors to view 300 to 400 stock prices without switching screens. Non-Life Insurance claims can be settled in a matter of hours and not over weeks and months as used to happen in the past.

The most remarkable thing about it is "presence". This is a deep visceral feeling of being there. Those who have experienced it recount memories of it as if it were a place they have visited—not something they saw on a screen. It is obviously a computer-generated world.

Naturally, the question arises as to the advantages of being there. Earlier the models used for viewing these things were operationally not quite suited for frequent use. Simpler versions have been developed and it is a cradle to slip a smart phone and use for viewing.

Samsung's Gear VR or Google's Cardboard are the play station versions with built-in displays and relies on external processing power. The uses of viewing range from entertainment, the thrill of being there, and more importantly for teaching, collaborations, or applications planned for future use.

The limitations of VR have drawn us to AR. AR is dependent on the outside world as it is. It senses depth and distance, crunches data about what they are looking at, and places objects in a correct position.

Distributed Ledger Technology

Generally Distributed Ledger Technology is referred to as Block Chain Technology. It is a shared database distributed across a network of individuals, organizations, and devices that maintains a growing list of transactions between participants. Transactional record is synchronized, each copy is identical and automatically updated. The data recorded is immutable and cannot be changed without the consent of all parties concerned. The development of smart contracts (business logic) is embedded in such distributed ledgers. It would not be wrong to say that a new functionality has been introduced.

For some unknown reasons, controversies and difficulties related to crypto currencies have encircled the developments of Block Chain Technology. What was supposed to be a major innovation, is currently in a state of suspended animation. One cannot however deny the fact that a number of fields are going to be influenced by putting to use this innovation.

The Financial Services Industry is now on the threshold of a major technological change. An outsider (say a Martian) visiting the present scene would well be reminded of the remarks of a valet of Louis XVI "Sire, it is not a revolt; it is a revolution."

Considerable investments, organizational restructuring, personalization of customer services, database decision making come to mind as major changes which are already in the pipeline. We would deal with them in detail when we look at specific segments and sectors of the Financial Services Industry.

In such a situation, large banks like the Seven Giants would have unique advantages. At the other end, a technical wizard could come out with solutions to handle the current problems and might affect Financial Company's Profit and Loss (P&L). In conversation with bankers we are often asked if this were the state of "Nirvana". The answer is categorical "No". Quantum computing is on the anvil and could overtake many of the changes being introduced now. We may be able to predict changes likely to come about during the next ten or fifty years. *Megatech—Technology In 2050*, a book by *The Economist*, does precisely that. However, it fails to point out as to when these changes could come about. We can know what kind of changes may come about but the most important aspect about its timing would be left hanging.

CHAPTER 3

The Internet: Engine for Change

One is indeed surprised that from a small beginning in 1969, the Internet which was primarily a channel for communication among researchers, was transformed into an integral system of our lives. It is not surprising that those who pioneered the Internet did not anticipate its development. The Internet usage has, since its inception, increased in a manner that could be described as phenomenal.

As a result of the very speed with which the Internet has developed and the rapid pace of change it has brought about we probably still do not understand the most important and far reaching implications; nor can we thoroughly anticipate the transformation the future has in store for us.

Eric Schmidt very aptly puts it as "The internet is the first thing that humanity has built that humanity does not understand—the largest experiment in anarchy that we have ever had. The perception of the internet to change our lives, the difficulty of predicting of how it would evolve, and its free anarchic barely controllable character combine to produce both real hope and a profound apprehension".

It would not be wrong to say that it has changed the very way we live. The rules for the whole economy stand completely changed.

Grassroots organizers adopted the Internet for political and social activism and used it to mobilize worldwide responses to natural disasters, human rights abuses and others. Users of all ages embraced the Internet as a medium for personal expression, and new applications helped democratize the technology by making it easier for ordinary people to

V. C. Joshi, *Digital Finance, Bits and Bytes*,
https://doi.org/10.1007/978-981-15-3431-7_3

independently produce and disseminate news, information, opinion, and entertainment.

However, many challenges remained as the Internet entered the twenty-first century. Users faced abusive practices such as spam (unwanted commercial E-mail), viruses, unidentified theft, and break-ins. Technical experts responded with solutions that attempted to minimize these ongoing dangers, providing anti-virus systems, filters, secure web transactions, and improved security systems. But other issues were too divisive for a technical solution to satisfy conflicting public opinion, especially when activities crossed national boundaries. Some governments severely limited and closely monitored the online activities of their citizens; while human rights groups protested this as censorship and intimidating surveillance, the governments in question asserted their right to prevent socially undesirable activities. The other technical issue with political ramifications was the proposed transition from the old Internet Protocol, called IPv4, to a new protocol called IPv6 that would provide a much larger number of addresses (Bradner and Mankin 1995); this was in part a response to the fact that the USA held a disproportionate share of the IPv4 addresses. IPv6 was proposed as an Internet standard in 1994, but due to technical and political disagreements the protocol was still only used for a tiny percentage of Internet traffic fifteen years later (DeNardis 2009). Given these many obstacles, the Internet's decentralized, consensus-based development process continued to work remarkably well to keep the system thriving amid rapid growth and change.

Perhaps most troubling was the persistent inequality of access to the Internet and its opportunities for economic development, political participation, government transparency, and the growth of local science and technology. Significant gaps remained between rich and poor regions, urban and rural citizens, and young and old. The United Nations reported in 2007 that the global digital divide was still enormous: "Over half the population in developed regions was using the Internet in 2005, compared to 9 per cent in developing regions and 1 per cent in the 50 least developed countries." (UN, 2007, 32.) To help address this issue, the UN and International Telecommunications Union sponsored a two-part World Summit on the Information Society in Geneva (2003) and Tunis (2005) to devise a plan of action to bring access to information and communication technologies to all of the world's people (WSIS 2008). Computer scientists also devoted their ingenuity to making the Internet more accessible to the world's poor.

No longer simply the domain of scientists, pushing the frontiers of the scientific developments, Internet increasingly involves social as well as technical innovation and much more than the collaboration of researchers, businesses, civil society organizations, governments, and ordinary people. The values guiding the Internet's social and technical development have been complementary: increasing access, accommodating diversity, decentralizing authority, making decisions by consensus with a wide range of participants, and allowing users to take an active role in adding features to the network. On the technical side, these goals have been achieved through layered architecture, open protocols, and a collaborative process for approving design changes, while social goals have been advanced through government leadership and the inspiration of individuals who saw the Internet's potential for communication, cooperation, and self-expression.

Table 3.1 shows the growth in number of users. We would also discuss these developments, the factors contributing to this growth phenomenon and its impact of Financial Services Industry.

The doctrine of globalization of trade and industry was [since 1985] gradually being put into practice. Many US, European, and even Japanese firms shifted part of their manufacturing activities to low wage countries. The needs of such companies under the earlier command and control systems of management necessitated global telecommunication network.

In the 1980s, officials of AT&T were reportedly saying that domestic and international markets could not be separated. They had accepted the needs of multinationals for telecommunication and data in a systematic and unified way. International solutions had to be found.

Table 3.1 Internet growth

	World Internet usage	
World regions	*Internet usage*	*Penetration rate (% population lac)*
Africa	492,762,185	37.3
Asia	2,197,444,783	51.8
Europe	719,365,521	86.8
Latin America & Caribbean	444,493,379	67.5
Middle East	173,543,542,069	67.2
North America	327,568,127	89.4
Oceania/Australia	28,634,278	68.4

Source: Nielsen Online and International Telecommunications Union. https://www.internetworldstats.com/stats.htm

The Internet was the need answered. About twenty years ago, connecting to the Internet meant "going" to the Internet. It was a peculiarly clumsy way of accessing it. The author vividly remembers sitting before his desktop, dialing a phone number and waiting patiently to get the connection for getting online. However, as everybody knows the last five to ten years have seen a phenomenal change. The Internet is all around us with ubiquitous WIFI dominating the field. It is such an accepted thing that one hardly even mentions it. It is like tap water, we would realize its importance when the pipelines burst or are shut off for some reason.

The FIs and the Internet

The financial services were bound to feel the impact of the new technology. The Financial Institutions even in less developed countries could not remain isolated from such changes. The customers' message in this behalf was loud and clear. These same customers did not favor using the brick-and-mortar distribution offices where they were "introduced" by their parents/grandparents. They needed anytime/anywhere seamless service. The FIs realized that core/legacy banking and insurance system could facilitate the introduction of online banking and insurance. Over a period, the institutions modified their systems so that the "know your customers" norms and, procedures for authentication were suitably modified in a manner that unhealthy practices like money laundering, cyber-attacks could be dealt with through new procedures and rules in this behalf. The attempt was to ensure that the new channel could be used to meet the client's requirements and at the same time to have a safe and secure channel. In some countries, to safeguard the client's interest, if a cyber-crime were reported to the client's branch within a stipulated period, the losses were made good. We elaborate this point in the chapter on Cyber-Risk Management (9).

During this period, the Internet was an "open" channel. Dan Schiller (Digital Capitalism: Networking the Global Market System, 2000) aptly summarizes the process of liberalization and shows how special policies were crafted to ensure that the sector was insulated from every kind of control but also provided with substantial public benefit. Gradually, during the late 1980s and 1990s one could see that what had originated as a specialized networking industry, endowed with exceptional market freedom was set to expand comprehensively into a great communication system. The liberalization process had outward rippling effect. The changes were such that it led to a comprehensive restructuring of world's infrastructure.

The Internet was and is built by utilizing a set of commands/protocols that enables the computers to setup an electronic space. The rights to use it were made freely available. Virtually nobody owned the network or made money from it directly.

It goes without saying that such expansion could not be achieved without huge IT investment. Companies like Boeing and General Motors were very keen on developing a company-wide information sharing culture so that their strategic capabilities were enhanced and productivity increased considerably. Research analysis carried out at diverse locations could reach the market with speed. The results could be shared very easily. To cut the story short, the supply end of the telecommunication industry comprised a strategic response to a shift in demand. Of course, the primary need was for preventing a crash of "mission control" data and for the data to slide smoothly.

It was necessary that the Internet should be "open". The White House document "The Framework of Global Electronics" envisages that the Internet should not be subject to governmental control. Additionally, in the legal domain the US Supreme Court judgment on the subject was also of great help. The judgment laid down that any laws to negate free speech through regulation of the Internet violated the constitutional provisions. In the opinion of some, this judgment was no less than a constitutional amendment for the twenty-first century. The New York Times very correctly mentions that "the judgement was so comprehensive that it was clear to anyone that any Government imposed restriction on Internet content would not be upheld as long as the matter had some constitutional value." It is in effect signaled that the government must not come in the way of the Internet and that regulatory measures should be minimal.

In fact, Banks and Commercial Enterprises lent all their might to ensure that such openness became an integral part of regulation in other countries also. The EU paper "Economic and Social Benefits of Internet Openness" states that "With its architecture open by design, its decentralized nature and its ubiquitous use, the internet is a powerful catalyst for innovation, economic growth, and social well-being and is the backbone of the digital economy."

By then it was an accepted doctrine that openness enables people to do more things online and this includes starting a business, creating new services, raising capital, sharing knowledge, communicating, and even conducting research.

In a Frequently Asked Questions (FAQ) type of analysis, it is stated that the Internet would/and thus facilitate innovation, entrepreneurship, and social well-being. Added to it was the global value chain and consequential international trade.

We have deliberately opened our analysis with the aspect of openness as it is this particular aspect which is today causing or is responsible for socio-political unrest and how to devise policies that would prevent activities of terrorists, socio-political groups within the country causing unrest, finance for illegal activities, and undue interference by countries in each other's affairs. There is every danger that it could be used for nefarious activities like money laundering also. Further, against the background of the current "nationalist policies" it is doubtful if the authorities would continue for long with such policies. There is a growing number of countries which have already imposed restrictions on the content to be distributed.

Further, the dominant position use of organizations like Amazon, Google, and Facebook, serious questions are about "privacy" or interfering in election processes and even in unhealthy economic competition; there is a great demand for regulatory measures.

To what extent would the new regulations allow free financial transactions is currently being vigorously debated. One senses considerable uneasiness about the openness question.

One very important aspect (often neglected) is the need through such means to guard the loyalty of customers. Customers in an "open" environment can shift their accounts for various services needed over a period of time. Needless to add that retaining customers and ensuring their loyalty to branch or brand is as important as acquiring new customer. Online buying is distinctly different from brick-and-mortar shopping. With the human intervention not being there, customer choices could be determined by any number of factors. Hence the need to see that the FI approach in dealing with such situations meet the requirements properly and adequately.

We now turn to examine the impact of another phenomenal development. It relates to the growth of Internet of Things (IoT).

Internet of Things

The Internet of Things (IoT) is the extension of the Internet connectivity to the physical devices and everyday objects. It makes objects recognizable to obtain intelligence and to communicate information about themselves. These objects can also access information that has been aggregated by other things. It allows people and things to be connected anytime, anyplace, with anything and anyone—ideally using any path/network and any service. It means it can deal with elements like conversions, content, collections, computing, and communication. According to Journal of IoT, IoT system is a network of networks where a massive number of objects, things, sensors, and devices are connected through communications and information infrastructure to provide value added services via intelligent data processing and management for different applications.

Basically, it refers to physical things in our daily use that would be connected to the Internet and would be able to identify themselves to other devices.

We show how banks and Financial Institutions could through this means collect information regarding their clients' behavior. IoT technology has empowered the finance industry in various ways to collect such information through sensor devices. The information thus collected could be used to assist the customers and help them to achieve better commercial result. We have in Chap. 2 shown how various devices contribute toward this end.

The Internet of Things is a veritable earthquake. It is as if the rules of physics are written on the fly. By 2020, there would be some 26 billion Internet connected devices. The new architecture will help us by functioning autonomously, creating self-aware systems out of our existing real world objects that will now monitor our readily available information environment and even improve it.

A cursory glance at the information thus available shows that it can help the FIs in launching predetermined and rightly timed targeted services. It would provide the personal touch necessary for marketing. It would lead to a highly proactive approach. The way the customers handled such apps could also point to a loop-hole from security perspective.

A varied set of applications like knowledge about geographical locations can help. A credit card company like Master Card can direct the users about the nearest store for purchase of groceries or other items. These results can readily be put in proper context. We must highlight the fact that FIs do not have that vantage position they enjoyed in the past. Reports show that customers have no hesitation in switching over from one institution to another and are prone to use services which appeared to be of considerable use and help at a given time. In the next three chapters we would bring out how intense the competition is. Even minor slip could be a step in bringing about the changes.

The importance of having information is determined by how effectively data analysis in respect of streaming information is undertaken. An insurance company which offers insurance for delays in flight departures and arrivals would need to be extremely prompt to credit customers' account with the amount of insurance. Various factors that need to be accounted for while settling the claim have to be activated and brought into play.

Search Engines

The contribution of search engines in the process of data generation and dissemination to those who want it (of course with due regard to regulation for safeguarding privacy) can be considerable. The search technologies offer information regarding number of clicks on a search button. The customers benefit as they can connect with the right suppliers and people, and have for their use exact details and information. It would not be wrong to say that search engines are cornerstones of the Internet technology. Following are some of the ways how this information could help suppliers and users or buyers:

- Saving of time
- Heightened awareness
- Aggregated price reviews
- Details regarding alternate avenues and opportunities available

In addition, the search engines could also generate information about its users that could benefit various other groups such as

- Retailers—locality wise
- Advertisers
- Information seekers
- Educational institutions and Government

Pricing of Internet Services

Very often we are bewildered by the questions of why and what we pay for Internet service. In the first place, the choice(s) before the customers are limited. Initially (at the time of the installation) one might get certain discounts, but subsequently these are discontinued.

Some of the following factors come into play. These are

- Customer inertia in shifting from one provider to another
- Promotion period pricing can be different from the long-term ones
- Initial discounts may get over and the customer could really shift if it is so desired, but rarely does it happen
- We very often forget that competition and price wars are quite prevalent in this sector
- Prices, usage tracking, and speed calculations are very often misleading

The best way to look at the question is to examine it through the suppliers' lens. The supplier lays the cables and builds the wireless towers in the hope that there would be a given number of users who would avail of that service. For the supplier the most important question is the recovery of these major costs.

We have to reckon with the fact that it is either duopoly or oligopoly pricing and that we have limited options to choose from. Further, once the cables are laid, the supplier has very little to do. All he has to take care of is to deal with some of the problems which customers may face. Some authors do point out that smart phones and 5G technology would totally change the picture. However, we are not sure. After all faster speeds come with higher prices. Increasingly we are getting to a situation where life without the Internet is hard to imagine. And the Internet providers know this!

Regulation of the Internet

We begin with a somewhat "text bookish" approach to this question. Obviously, there are as many approaches to this question as there are people to express their views on. There are some who advocate total ban and punishment for the providers and content developers. Others advocate empowering the police and enforcement agencies to track down all those who create such objectionable content.

However, an objective analysis shows that regulation is a whole process of control or guidance by established rules and procedures applied by the regulators like governments or administrative authorities. It therefore has an interventionist connotation based on "public interest" goals. There are always different ways to handle this matter. It could begin with self-regulation and could end with the creation of a regulatory body to oversee the activity. Coupled with legal authorities, the regulators can effectively undertake this function.

At the present juncture, these issues have a unique importance from political point of view. Interference through fake advertisements or news during the election process by foreign powers is assuming considerable importance. Since the companies like Facebook/Google are dependent on advertisement revenues they find it difficult to safeguard the wider social interest. Similarly distributing "terrorist material" or providing information for financing such activities also are given publicity. Politically motivated false messages could have serious impact.

The objectives like respect for public mores, taste, and observing cultural standards have receded into the background. The "reach" and customer/client base of the corporations like Facebook and Google is such that their activities can be considered to be global. Levying fines even in billions hardly affects such corporations. Therefore, there is a clamor to break up these units and subject them to continuous scrutiny. In a limited sense the earlier rules and regulations on child pornography, and so on, are still prevalent and do need to be rigidly implemented. Add to this protection of personal privacy issues. Unknowingly we append our signatures to disclosure agreements and these could lead to totally unintended results. The best course in these circumstances would be a blanket denial.

In the case of Internet, the absence of a central organization is a big stumbling block. The nature of Internet content is similar to that of newspapers, broadcasting, or even a library system. It is an international medium with a very loose international management. Currently, their main work seems to be registration of domain names.

One is always faced with constant technology innovations that need to be brought under the purview of the regulatory authorities. The size and the breadth of these activities lead to divergent responses. Ranging from strict controls to a total freedom and the free market economics option are constantly being debated on.

The technical innovation at times needs to be discarded as the removal of old rules (no longer applicable) and introduction of newer ones is a time-consuming process. In such situations, it is not surprising to find that regulators pleading inability because of the changing environment.

Technical openness increases when openly available protocols are used consistently to receive and send data flows. Economic openness varies with the ability of individuals to get online and to enhance their economic opportunities. Social openness is related to the use of Internet to broaden non-pecuniary opportunities.

The openness of the Internet has enabled platforms and tools to transfer tacit knowledge, thus spurring innovation. A report for the configuration of Swedish Enterprise concludes that openness facilitates exchange of knowledge, ideas, interests, and view-points on a broad scale.

However, one must realize that it can also facilitate unauthorized access to personal data, violations of privacy rights, and/or digital security breaches.

We have seen the way this openness has been used for misleading propaganda and spread of terrorist ideology. There can be grave consequences and unintended results. It would be useful to add that the developments in Egypt (the Arab Spring) have somehow misled people into believing that the Internet could well become a facilitator for expressing resentment, anger, and so on against dictators and could pave the way for the establishment of democratic governments. Unfortunately, developments in 2016 in USA and elections in Ukraine and even in France showed that the Internet can be thoroughly misused. Even Facebook shared the data with Cambridge Analytica and the most undesirable manipulations took place.

Some thinkers and self-styled champions of freedom are preaching a completely hands-off approach.

The speed, scale, and connectedness have been facilitated by modern technology. The capacity to capture data means we can conduct almost all our financial transactions with the help of the Internet. The cumulative impact would be increased transparency and, capacity to capture data means we can expect transformation in every aspect, creativity, efficiency, and stability. Eric Schmidt in the "NEW Digital Age" rightly tells us to expect transformation in every aspect.

Al Gore puts it very succinctly. "*The internet has spawned new types of capital flows and consumer markets, and that we are witnessing the explosive growth of new models, social organizations and patterns of behavior that would have been unimaginable before the internet.*"

It would not be wrong to say that while various devices come our way, the regulatory authorities cannot be expected to keep pace with them. Theoretical and normative frameworks employed to deal with such changes are not always able to move at a speed warranted by the circumstances. The horizons that have opened up are wide and so new that they could be considered as unheard of. It is likely that entirely new economic flows can and do actually emerge. A smart chair could be sold without any charge. The manufacturers of such smart chairs would then get their money back through recommendations on the problems your back might suffer. They could advise the purchaser on the monthly basis regarding his/her posture, and so on.

We sum up with a quotation from Rifkin, third Industrial Revolution Prophet. "The world is increasingly shaped by Digital Prophets.!! The whole thing is premised on the idea that social media, big data, and hyperactive algorithms have fundamentally altered the ways in which we socialize, amuse ourselves, learn about the world, act politically, and do business. The Internet is not merely the backbone for doing business or infrastructure for economic transactions, but the very oxygen that allows us to innovate, collaborate, produce, and exchange goods and services."

So far, we have looked at the question from an organizational perspective. We now look at some advantages which the customers would have. A question that often comes up is regarding the spread of the Internet. How did the Internet become entrenched as a business infrastructure? How has the Internet got acceptance on such a wide scale? Does it help in building trust?

We also have to look at the macro-economic consequences of the Internet. The Banks/Insurance companies have always aspired to spread their wings on global market. The crucial part of the argument was that the customers wanted us to be in those locations. For the banks even in less developed countries, the preferred destination was London. The Internet facilitated the expansion.

Secondly, as pointed out by Dan Schiller "Big Banks have transformed throughout the past decade to constitute a concentrated and diversified industry processing a multifaceted global reach. Large multi nationals offer diverse services. They made the services available all over their branch network. They undertook massive investments in information technology [credit/Debit cards]." Greater share of work was in data processing and telecommunications. At the same time Head offices/Zonal offices could exercise effective control and monitor some high-risk business The Author when he operated at an overseas center found that whenever he had to undertake somewhat riskier transactions, he could always get the Head office to help him in reaching a desired solution.

Further a number of innovative approaches could be developed and quickly became embedded in the system. In securities trading high frequency trading was becoming the norm. Saving even a few milliseconds could earn the entity huge gains. Further a door was opened to improve on product design and reduction in labor costs.

The Internet's function as a critical business infrastructure was surpassed by its importance as a site of commodification, that is, as a site for newer industries capable of generating newer avenues for profit.

We briefly touch on growth of wearables and Internet of things. They have sensors embedded in roads, plants, equipment, and consumer goods. These appliances have unique Internet addresses to enable machine to machine communications. Devices connected to the Internet are expected to outnumber humans by ten to one. They create huge data and through analysis could make available valuable information.

We would briefly refer to software as a free and open service [Free and open source Software]. The software required had to develop a character of a public good like air. This was a response to some inner urge and facilitated by almost the global reach of these developers. In the networked environment information could be created by a group of volunteers without being paid for their services. They have solved the public goods problem in a way that they do not have to close it and charge a fee. The availability of an innovative group of creators/users to guide developers was the free largescale collaboration. They could thus develop approaches which were/are far more complex than originally envisaged.

One can easily see that costs for such development, for [mutual benefit], would have been too high. Through such cooperation it is reduced almost to zero.

More at unit level we find

1. Decentralization of conceptions and execution of problems
2. Harnessing of diverse talents

3. Separation of management and governance through hierarchies could be through selection and discussions.

We should appreciate that that complexity and uncertainty make information problems of matching people, resources, and projects less amenable to mere managerial intervention/or even being price based.

A system that allows agents to explore their universe for problems, solutions, and experiments to learn and to iterate on their solutions and refinement without requiring intermediate formalization to permit and fund the process will obviously have an advantage over a system that requires these formalizations.

We now briefly touch on the emergence of an altogether a novel way of conducting transactions without the banks as intermediaries. Basically, E-finance refers to using the Internet as a platform to provide banking services, secure banking, insurance policies, and the link as well as to the computer network for technical support of the financial activities. Mobile payment, cloud computing social networking and such engines will have a fundamental impact on the human financial model that is different from indirect financing by banks. In the Chinese model there is no intermediary but the two sides allocate the resources directly through the network to match supply and demand.

It is rightly feared that Internet finance may replace traditional finance and may impact the banks in a big way. Some even believe in the banks' disappearance as a possibility.

Banks traditionally mobilize savings and optimize investments. They improve the efficiency of allocation of funds. Commercial banks, in the traditional model are important bridges to promote such allocation. In the Internet model the lender and the borrower decide on these matters without any intermediary. The result could be financing for high risk clients.

We must touch on another important aspect having a bearing on this subject. In China deposit rates are decided on by the Government. The rates are low and lead an aggressive client to look for greener pastures. They have neither the banks to support them nor the government rescue them.

CHAPTER 4

E-Insurance

Chapters 4, 5 and 6 would deal with E-Insurance, E-Banking, and E-Trading respectively. The attempt would be to see how insurers, bankers, and traders meet the challenges emanating from the emergence of disruptive technologies, cut throat competition, and changing profile of their customers, particularly the millennials and the other younger groups. All these entities are faced with the need to absorb newer technologies, deal with the high staff costs, on account of induction of highly skilled staff (say, data analyst), and the vastly different socio-economic environment. Almost everywhere the FSIs are faced with these problems and there are varied ways in which they have tried to meet these changes. There are, no doubt, a number of similarities and one can discern quite a few common elements.

As if all these problems were not enough, the institutions had to start with regaining the lost/dented trust of their customers. The technology front saw the emergence of Fintech and Insurance technology (InsuTech) firms which had begun to develop financial products and were about to attack the soft underbelly and grab a share in the profitable segments. The customers were also becoming restless and wanted MARTINI (the old drink advertisement talked of anywhere anytime) insurance/banking facilities. Further they did not need handholding services offered by brokers/agents. Their unhappiness with siloed branches was quite apparent and they wanted seamless services through their mobile and smart phones.

V. C. Joshi, *Digital Finance, Bits and Bytes*,
https://doi.org/10.1007/978-981-15-3431-7_4

For the sake of convenience, we deal with these aspects separately but action has to be initiated on these fronts simultaneously. Trust could be regained through prompt settlements and avoidance of small print exclusions in the policies to the extent possible. Further, institutions had to reinvent their core values and strict adherence to regulatory requirements and constantly make efforts to fulfill customer expectations. The customer pays his/her premium with the belief that if they did business with a certain company, they would get the value of that business even at a later date.

Customer experience is at the root of that belief. Business will be experience-driven and the expected results would be making the customers' lives easier and better. The process of underwriting, servicing the policies, and settling of claims that may come up creates a number of touch points. The companies that can make the journey smooth and seamless would have an advantage and edge over their competitors.

Innovations referred to earlier are a key driver of the changes in the financial sector. Some companies in the insurance sector have taken advantage of such developments and have achieved significant results. No doubt, a certain amount of uncertainty does prevail during the initial stages. The financial service industry deals in intangible products and is obviously suited for innovations. The basic idea is to lower costs, develop new products to meet customer requirements, emerging out of new shared economy products (Uber, Airbnb) or emergence of newer risks. The major developments can be attributed to the following:

- Proliferation of Internet Connections
- Home Computing
- Mobile Devices
- Development of Applications leading to lowering of barriers for market entry
- These innovations lead to new methods of service provision, data collection, and these lead to better identification of risks and mitigation measures. These are referred to as "InsuTech" as opposed to FinTech which is used primarily in banking.

It must be said that these changes have so far, not received a wide spread acceptance. A number of insurers in response to PWC Survey on Risks have admitted that "Management of Change" is their major worry and that they consider that as risk number one for the industry. It might be pertinent to add that in the emerging scenario we can distinctly notice two strands namely those who have accepted the innovations and are moving on and those who are grappling with basic problems, like coming up with solutions for meeting emerging demands but continue to operate with legacy systems.

We referred to Uber and Airbnb in an earlier paragraph. Commercial Motor Liability Insurance is a requirement for taxi drivers; it may not cover Uber as they are part time drivers. The need for products on demand poses challenges to insurers as never before. Cyber-risk is one such area; the attacks do pose newer problems practically all the time and a need for another product covering the risk emerges. Actuaries have to come up with innovations and changes almost on an hourly basis. In the final analysis, the insurance companies have to come out with products to cover new risks that cannot possibly fit the traditional life style or economic activity responses. Before considering the changes that have been brought in, we briefly review the technologies that have been put to use.

1. Mobile Technologies and Applications

The network effect of mobile phones and development of applications for these devices has allowed many companies to reach larger number of customers [potential and actual] than was previously possible. Mobile networks that allow short messages as well as data transfers have made it possible for the companies to notify individuals on anything from premium to withdrawal of air time for premium payments. Further contacting the customers is much easier. Distance is no bar.

2. Algorithms and Robot Advisers

Before proceeding further, we have to highlight the fact that the developments and use of Internet have reduced the need for brokers/agents. The customer deals directly with the companies and gradually the intermediaries are being eliminated. Before proceeding further, we briefly touch on some of the factors that have facilitated the use of AI and ML in financial services. The last twenty years have seen a number of changes which could be considered as contributory factors.

- Cost of Computing has declined considerably
- Power of Computing has increased considerably

- Wearable Devices have created large databases required to feed AI engines
- Data Usage depends on intelligent support
- ML makes systems adaptable
- Technology base is growing exponentially

AI refers to the ability of a computer or a computer installed robot system to process information and produce outcomes in a manner similar to the thought processes of humans. By extension the goal of the AI systems is to tackle complex problems in ways similar to human logic and reasoning. (See PWC Hype or Hope.) The goal of the AI systems, as stated earlier, is to deal with complex problems. The main features can be stated as under:

- Learn from experience
- Use the learning to reason
- Recognize images
- Understand language nuances
- Create perspectives

At the intersection of the adjacent domains, automation is playing out on many fronts.

- Automation of Trust (block chain)
- Automation of Insight (machine learning)
- Automation of Awareness (natural languages)
- Automation of Recognition (computation vision)

The main threat for FIs comes from the fact that their products can be decomposed and dealt with as separate products.

It would be useful to state that machines could be considered intelligent when they act to maximize the possibility of achieving a given goal. AI research is taking place in fields that include reasoning, planning, learning, and even natural language processing. The robot advisers are also aggregators who take the place of intermediaries.

In the field of insurance, it is particularly useful for quotes and offerings calculated through algorithms. It can provide automated guidance and execution on various financial decisions. The clients could get advice for most of their queries. Exceptional problems can easily be handled by investment advisers. The need for brokers—intermediaries could arise for the thin file customers who could be described as inclusive insurance schemes (micro insurance etc.).

Smart Contract

Any contract which is capable of enforcing itself and written as programming code and which can run on a computer rather than in legal terminology is a smart contract. It defines rules and consequences that emulate a legal document stating obligations, benefits, and penalties due to either party being in different circumstances.

The efforts in this behalf had to be in all the segments because the overall environment was undergoing a change. These processes were to an extent helped by development of "Applications" which helped in lowering the entry barriers. The innovations led to new ways of service provisions, new methods of data collection, and to better identification of risks and mitigation methods.

Technology Challenge

It must not be assumed that merely because these things were happening, there was a rush for adaptions to these changes. The softest option was to see if the immediate challenges could be met through additions to or modifications to the existing platforms. It was perhaps thought that adding another layer would suffice as in the past such services could be rendered by these methods. In the process, the technology structure was like the layers in a piece of cake. Prof. Weill's famous remarks dubbing the structure as "Spaghetti Platform" has gained wide spread acceptance. These platforms were rigid and turned out to be insufficient and could not fulfill the purpose for which they were to be used now.

As mentioned earlier, these technology developments were described as disruptive. The very use of the term suggests that the newer technology has a rapid and major effect on the business activities and the processes that existed before. The innovations displaced the existing technology and shook the industry and led to creation of new products with a view to compete with the companies by undercutting their old products and weaning away their customers.

We begin by looking at the way insurers and bankers responded to the emerging challenges. The choice about technology transformation can and does vary from organization to organization. However, in the case of insurance and banks, we see two different trends in the development. In the case of banking, the innovators turned out to be disruptors in conformity with the Authors' definition and tried to take away profitable portion of bank's business. Payments and money transfers and other fee income constituted nearly 29% of banking industries profit and the FinTech companies did try to enter these businesses.

However, many of these companies could not engage in turf wars. The smaller entities suffered from lack of capital funds and could not match the banks' customer base. They were only too willing to merge with the banks so that they could grow under the regulatory umbrella. In the next chapter we go on to show how there was a close fit and the advantages through big data, machine learning and so on made all the difference.

The insurance industry however did not have to worry about InsuTech units straddling their turf or cutting into their profitable businesses. We therefore have to deal with some very important questions about the active collaboration with the insurers as against the somewhat adversarial relations with FinTechs in banking.

We raised this matter with the senior executives (past and present) and did get the following response.

- The insurance industry took a calculated step and financed InsuTech firms. They set up venture capital funds (VC Funds). These VC Funds financed almost 60%of investments e.g. Munich Re has made substantial investments in an on-demand insurance provider company.
- The insurance industry business model is somewhat complicated. The "retained" business with a given insurer could be about 1%, while the rest would be covered by reinsurers. Such sharing depends on a critical evaluation by the reinsurers of various aspects of their working and more particularly of various dimensions of "underwriting" processes and practices. It would not be wrong to say that risks are specific and even under similar circumstances could lead to different conclusions. The reinsurers and large sized brokers do have a better knowledge of the risks and the companies stand to gain through their mediation.
- Insurance regulatory norms are very rigidly adhered to.
- Claim settlement does vary from case to case.
- The industry had to carry on and undertake some activities like motor insurance though they are loss making. The investment port-

folios of the insurance industry helped in absorbing such losses. During the crisis, AIG got involved in some terribly risky investments and was on the verge of collapse. Were it not for Government help, it would have been difficult to save them.

- The insurance companies had a huge database and they could easily integrate (through analytics) the information gained in their pricing or product decisions. The InsuTech companies could never match these trends. The tech companies were never able to match insurers in this respect.

It would, at this stage, be necessary to see how some of the insurance companies were remodeling their systems and procedures, and even had a re-look at their corporate objectives. The insurance industries' acceptance of the need for a radical departure is particularly noteworthy.

The additional fact that customers were easily able to gather information through social media or through aggregators was an important factor. Further, once the premiums were paid, the customers tended to be loyal customers and as such at the initial stage, pricing decisions and product features have considerable importance. The cumulative impact of technologies like block chain, AI, ML are now becoming the accepted tools for the insurance industries to conduct their activities. Basically, there are four main aspects that need to be looked into while setting the objectives. These could be described as under:

- Product design
- Pricing and Underwriting
- Distribution and Administration
- Claims Management

These were the prime concerns. Pricing which was largely an actuarial exercise ceased to be so. Modifications in response to market conditions and competition had to be undertaken—no doubt reluctantly. Insurers are now moving toward customized usage based on real time coverage model and are adopting prices in proportion to risk management. With the gradual replacement of brokers and branch development managers, the industries try and make it a point to meet customers' requirements of anywhere any time services. AR and VR coupled with seamless billing via mobiles have brought major changes. Jacquis Griffiths in his paper of January 2018 refers to an observation by the director of Microsoft for insurance:

"non-industry entrants and FinTech innovations provide increasing choice and raise customer expectations for frictionless personalized experience". We have already pointed out the important part played by big data analysis and it is increasingly being used for product differentiation. The insurers are responding with automated channels and perhaps 40% of the customers whose requirements are met through automated channels come under this category. Chatbots using natural languages provide the required particulars. While multiple stake holders are involved in a policy, insurers need to insure for real time provision of an immutable audit trails and block chains provide the solution.

Another key driver for insurers to maximize the value of their data, is risk modeling. An increasingly unpredictable risk environment combined with regulatory changes make risk management the perpetual focus for insurers. They need to be confident that they can respond quickly to an unexpected event and that they can assess the impact of these opportunities bring. Such analysis is possible only through insights obtained from data analysis in real time.

The cloud provides an agile, scalable, and flexible technology foundation to improve overall modeling capabilities, better response to regulatory pressures, better models, and anticipated risks. By leveraging high performance computing in the cloud, insurers are achieving levels of risk modeling that were not possible before.

The biggest innovation in insurance over the next three years will not be technology tools but how we design them with customers, agents, employees, and other human partners. These principles are being put into practice as the insurance industry leverages its advantages through AI, IoT, and cloud technologies. To get complete advantages from these, the insurers need to develop agile, profitable, and competitive business.

We have earlier referred to procedural changes made by the insurance industry. For a long time, insurance has been associated with a degree of frustration. Their underwriting processes to a lengthy experience of claim settled, a total lack of data analysis being used to personalize and tailor the customer experience was the cause of such frustration.

Customer expectations have changed dramatically. Insurance is based largely on trust. The customer pays a subscription believing that if they do business with a certain company, they should get the value of that business later. Customer experience is at the root of that trust and the large part of today's experience has to come from technology usage.

With an increasing amount and rising costs, the way business was done formerly could not cut ice any longer. Insurance companies had to make lives of their customers easier and better with their technologies. There are multiple touch points for attracting customers, and underwriting the risks effectively, handling claims, and maintaining a long-term relationship are some of these. Companies that excel in all these phases will enjoy a significant competitive advantage for customer growth and profitability.

Further, as stated earlier, many of these companies find it difficult to keep pace with market demands. They are not able to bring out products quickly when the market demand changes. Cyber-security insurance products, shared economy products readily come to mind. The actuarial departments are not able to formulate (for want of required data) new schemes that cover the emerging risks. Such problems about "adequate" versus large data requirements are bound to occur and do occur in other areas also. Big data analysts everywhere are grappling with these problems. And there are no easy solutions.

Sharing Economy

The sharing economy (Uber car drivers, Airbnb residences) are posing peculiar problems to the insurance sector. The question was how to handle liability insurance for an automated vehicle or for a driver who is working only for the time he drives a customer. Similarly, the insurance required by an Airbnb renter is for the time that the renter uses the rented premises.

Providing insurance cover for these peculiar situations became possible because of provisions of technology gadgets in vehicles and residences. Automobiles are jammed with sensors, back-up cameras, blind spot detectors, and computer technologies such as touch screens etc. As one insurer put it, you are no longer driving a car, you are driving a computer. Today, technology has taken care to see that everything is insured. In fact, even drones are being used to determine how, where, and when adjusters should be sent whenever disaster hits.

There are number of companies which have yet to make the required changes on the technology front. They are perhaps trying to see if the existing technologies could stand them in a good stead or if they could wait and study the emerging picture before venturing forth. In addition to having a look at the technology platforms these companies would also need to have a hard look at the changing customer profile and the business content.

We would now review how the recent technology advances and collaborations with FinTech companies is working up. There is no doubt a distinct change in corporate objectives. There is altogether a new flavor to the insurance companies working. Many of them identify their purpose as "empowering" people to lead better lives and therefore better living partnerships. This does however, by no means mean that they are immune to the rough weather being encountered on account of intense competition among existing companies and new entrants.

The problems of technology upgradation are very much there. The current thrust seems to be on AI and Robotics. This in our view seems to be a right response to mitigating the regulatory requirements, risk management, and need for upgradation on products and introduction of newer ones. The environment they encounter and their current business needs, the considerable reliance on AI and ML is certainly justifiable. There is an acute need to teach their staff to work in sync with robots and get to a situation where through ML the robots do act responsibly. We are told that they expect to have humans working along with robots in the next two to three years.

At the same time, they have to integrate AR and VR capabilities with their software. Some of the training managers, report that formerly they had to take their surveyors to stay in an affected area. With VR, they can, in the classroom itself demonstrate 6/8 likely scenarios in the settlement process.

Innovative ideas impacting pricing decisions are now being put into practice. Every time a smoker opens up his mobile, his face as affected by smoking and drinking does come up. Plans for healthy living automatically get made known and the fees are scaled upward or downward depending on client's behavior. It is clear that technology is now used to build up partnership not only with customers but with staff etc.

The impact on productivity is equally important. Automation is no longer restricted to back offices but now covers front line customer service. The companies now expect that surveyors and others aided by technology should be able to settle claims in a few hours or as some officials put it, in minutes instead of doing it over days as is the current practice. "Teaching" AI propelled machines to act "responsibly" is now the company's main challenge.

It is necessary to point out that Data Analytics gets somewhat vitiated because of inherent biases. The only way to dispel such implicit biases and turn decision making as objective as possible, is to make the process transparent. This would lead to using a further extension to data that is "Extended Reality".

One thing is clear. Insurance companies need to have a vision and a well-drawn out road map for achieving these goals. Once it is in place, harnessing the right technology would follow.

We have so far concerned ourselves with only the technology problems. These factors also affect the industry in other ways and these are reviewed in what follows.

The increase in volume of electronic data, the ubiquity of mobile interfaces and continuous use of AI and so on would lead to a paradigm shift in total working. The insurance ecosystem is an interconnected set of services that allows users to fulfill a variety of needs in one integrated experience. Consumer ecosystems currently emerging tend to concentrate on needs such as travel, health care, housing, and so on. B2B ecosystems revolve around certain decision makers and marketing and sales operation, procurement, and financing professions can be dealt with available software. McKinsey consultants are suggesting that by 2025, about 12 ecosystems would emerge and should satisfy fundamental human needs (mobility, housing, health, wealth, and welfare protection). It is necessary to elaborate and to say that ecosystems would provide three types of values:

- They provide a gateway. Customers can switch over to related services.
- They would harness network effects
- They integrate data across a series of services.

Currently insurance brokers and agents act as aggregators. Henceforth with aggregators coming in, they stand exposed to disintermediation and disaggregation. They have a somewhat passive relationship with customers. They thus stand exposed to disintermediation and disaggregation. It would then be difficult for them to get back their customers once again.

Insurers not only have a strong database but have already a healthy collaboration with FinTech. They are advanced AI users and can easily adapt to the data emanating from IoT. Further, the claim settlements are becoming faster and more and more date driven.

They thus have to constantly examine and reexamine, their customer relationships, partnerships, and emerging competition. In short, technology and talent have to be enmeshed. Insurance companies do have enough resilience and achieve these.

MICRO INSURANCE

Micro Insurance was on the front burner during the 1970s but seems to have receded into background for some time now. Development economists and thinkers have been advocating that micro insurance for the poorer sections of the society is a must. Pioneers in various parts of the world had been with their daring vision propagating that micro insurance is a must for poverty alleviation. One must admit that without their vision, it would not have been possible as is being done now.

Micro Insurance can be defined either with reference to the quantum of insurance provided or with coverage for like health care insurance for the poor or crop damages insurance for small and marginal farmers. For quite some time, there seems to be a confusion arising from massive aid flows for major disasters. There is no doubt that but for such aid from various agencies, rehabilitation of poor and affected would never have been possible. Even in cases of fires in multistory buildings, part of the expenses for rehabilitation is met by voluntary donors. It is therefore felt by some theorists that such aid could well be regarded as a part of micro insurance.

These expenses would be beyond the abilities of insurance companies. Lloyds of London have come up and said that reinsurance claims on account of climatic changes or other factors are virtually making their normal work impossible.

We are of the view that expenses of such nature need not be considered under micro insurance. We must segregate such aid from normal insurance requirements for the poor. In view of the fact that there is a growing body of people who because of the frequency of such requirements are not happy with such aid being offered. Gradually governments, insurance companies, and bankers will have to come forward and take care of such needs. Such requirements for aid are not restricted only to very poor Asian or African countries. Fires in USA, flooding in other parts of the world, excessive snow falls are now problems encountered in developed countries also.

The scope of micro insurance needs to be restricted to claims coming under hospitalization expenses for illness, minor operations (expenses for health insurance), accidents, or other hazards affecting a family or few families. Depending on probability studies limits for amounts insured could well become the criteria for micro (Inclusive Insurance could be a better term) under this category. It is worth noting that the insurance regulatory authority in India has prescribed a limit of Rs. 50,000/- for policies to be classified under the Inclusive Insurance category.

For the sake of clarity in definition, we look at two strands of micro insurance pertaining to social security needs/benefits and the other like health insurance. In the past a major factor hindering the development of micro insurance was the cost of transactions. Insurance like its banking counterpart, was a labor-intense industry. The expenses per transaction therefore appears to be disproportionate to the premium earned. With the increase in wage bills, it was not feasible for insurers to undertake this activity. Firms undertaking such business were actually losing moneys in the process.

Thanks to FinTech developments, what was an "out of bounds" activity has now reached the possibility of being a profitable business channel. It is our considered view that unless insurance and banking companies include this work as part of their normal business model, it would be treated as being part apart. We are therefore led to say that this work has to be a normal integral part of their working.

Broadly, micro insurance covers both rural and urban populations. Right from health insurance to death of an earning member, to loss of crops, animal husbandry needs to be covered. Vast majority of people are not aware of such facilities being available. The reasons for it are not far to seek.

- Day to day needs take priority
- Lack of information and financial awareness
- Suitability of tailored products

The income generating assets could be the human beings involved, farm products, tools, tractors, pumps, and other equipment and even livestock. The insurable needs thus are very complex. Further these needs have to be covered almost annually. A great effort for follow-up and persuasion would be necessary. In the following sections we briefly touch on methods and measures proposed for meeting these needs.

We now state that far greater success could be achieved if banks, insurance companies, and FinTechs were to join hands and work together. It may sound like a dogmatic assertion that unless the companies look on these activities as an integral part of their business model, chances of succeeding would be far less. We are aware that this suggestion could be thrown out as being impractical, but our field experience leads us to believe that such collaborative effort is necessary if scarce public savings (particularly in less developed countries) are to be put to proper use. As trustees it is the duty of these institutions to safeguard these scarce resources in such risky endeavors.

The core elements of micro insurance can be diagrammatically represented in Fig. 4.1.

The poorer households when exposed to financial shocks (arising from accidents, illnesses, etc.) are generally forced to make very harsh choices such as

- Reducing food consumption
- Not paying school fees/removing children (particularly girls) from school
- Depleting productive assets to cover the expenses related to risk event

The spread of micro insurance is indeed very encouraging. It plays a very important role in overcoming poverty and benefits can go beyond mere health cycles. Even children stay longer in schools and are able to pursue their studies better.

In rural areas to meet conditions of drought or floods, companies tend to make lumpsum payments. However, with the availability of big data, index-based insurance could be a more appropriate solution. We do not

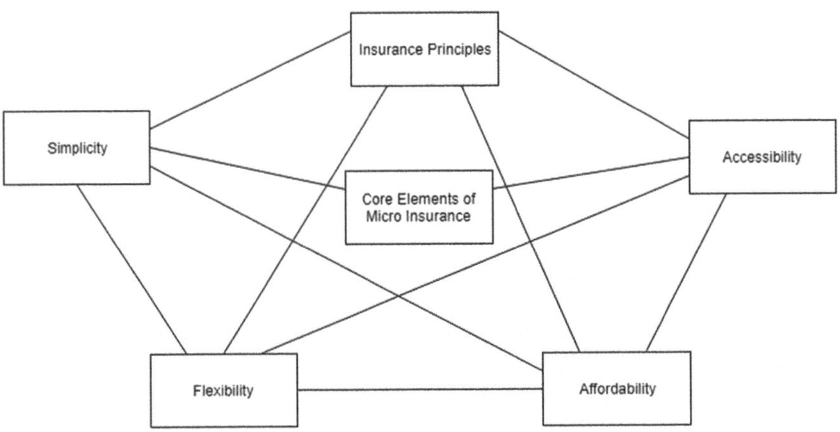

Fig. 4.1 Elements of micro insurance. (Source: Swiss RE—Economic Research and Consulting)

wish to go into details of preparing such schemes for settlement of claims but field officers have told us that wherever they have used these methods (somewhat crude though they are at this stage) they have had better results. In fact, there is a feeling that needs for insurance in rural areas could be better met in this way and perhaps provide the answer for sustainable business.

The problem is delivering insurance to almost the billion people below the poverty line. Micro Insurance is a business and not a charity. Insurers have therefore to find ways to reach customers in the remote and inaccessible parts of less developed countries. Currently, profits may not be very high but the potential is for significant returns at a later date. Today's low-income customer could be a high-income consumer of tomorrow. At this stage, the need is basically for two products—health and life insurance. Unfortunately, while one part of the country may suffer from floods, another could be reeling under droughts. Therefore, innovative insurers who welcome a challenge and have eyes on long-term strategy stand to benefit.

We must realize that risk materializes in various forms causing damage to life, health of individuals, to households, business assets, or public infrastructure. Insurance can fulfill the following functions:

- From a livelihood perspective, it could support resilience
- It helps faster recovery. The insured are not required to depend on coping strategies
- Policy holders would have a degree of peace of mind and could be induced to adopt improved techniques
- Insurers can nudge people to take preventive measures
- Lastly perhaps insurance facilitates better management of unexpected risks.

The development so far indicates that gradually the focus is shifting to "inclusive insurance". The focus has shifted from supporting merely micro insurance to even families who could be thrown back into poverty without insurance. These are vulnerable groups and are liable to suffer from even climate risk.

A holistic financial system would mean starting with a diagnostic approach and building the capacities and lastly measuring achievements in making insurance inclusive. Integrating insurance markets into national strategies would be a key to far superior performance. It is expected that the performance of insurance companies could be measured through renewal rates and claims settlements. Another allied sector which would also profit comprises the small and family business activities. Some companies would also like to couple small and medium sized business activities in these groups. The advantages for the medium and small enterprises are shown in the Table 4.1.

We now look at micro insurance particularly in the agriculture sector.

Micro insurance is of great importance to the growth of agricultural sector. It helps producers to stabilize their income and to respond to larger weather risks or floods and fires. Micro insurance for crops would be benefitted if index-based approached (referred earlier) were used to make payments based on easily observable indices related to crop yield outcomes. Compared to crop insurance, index-based approaches have the potential to address more effectively the difficulties of small farmers. The most common source of information, for developing index-based insurance is its linkages to crop yields.

In the field of agriculture, many of the customers are first time buyers with specific needs and equally specific consumption patterns. Insurance industry will have to build trust and even awareness by consistently demonstrating its value.

Traditional models may not work and would turn out to be too expensive. Mobile technology could help in distribution. It is here that Insurance Tech companies could assist in reaching a large body of emerging consumers. Micro Ensene and BIMA are based on use of mobile technology. It is equally important to see that the companies are not impeded by legacy of outdated systems, high cost of production, lack of product innovation, or the required focus on pushing sales. Even the younger generation in poorer families have expectations similar to those youngsters in metropolitan areas.

Table 4.1 Advantages of medium and small enterprises

Increasing resilience	Spurring investments
Sensitizes for better risk management	Encourages investments in slightly higher risky opportunities
Reduces dependence on costly risk coping strategies	Opens up new funding opportunities
Sustains productivity and promotes faster recovery	Freeze up existing funds

Source: Author

Table 4.2 Digitization in insurance sector

Marketing	*Pricing and underwriting*	*Product management*	*Claims handling*	*Customer interaction*
• Customer specific targeted markets • Robot advice chatbots • Internet sales price comparison • Social media smart phone channels	• Automated product service • Big data enabled activity • Predict customer wants • Continuous real time communication	• Platform in business models • 360° view of customer • Continuous real time data focus on high value	• Better risk understanding • Granular pricing • Block chain technology • Potential pricing data	• Fraud detection • Belief chain trustworthy and time of claims information • Smart phone lodgments of claims • Supply chain management efficiencies

Source: McKinsey digitization and insurance value chains

For the sake of easy reference, we illustrate in Table 4.2 the process of digitization in the insurance sector. The reader could at a glance have the complete process in view. This table analyzes the elements that are likely to be encountered under a digitized marketing plan. The customer is better informed and insurer is aware of competitor's prices and exclusions if any.

To summarize, one notices two distinct responses to the technology disruption taking place. On one hand, certain companies give the impression that they have responded to these challenges through a collaborative effort and that the transition had been smooth and easy. The changes have facilitated a considerable re-orientation of their activities and that it is a smooth and easy one. On the other hand, in a survey of risks facing the insurance industry globally, (Banana skins 2017 PWC) brings out the fact that the legacy systems, the expenses involved in replacement, and in general management of change is a great risk facing the insurance industry. There is a great reluctance emerging out of profit and loss consideration on making the necessary changes. Because of the heavy costs involved, the status quo with all the concomitant problems is sought to be maintained.

Over the last three years, some of the insurers have accepted the fact that they need to adapt to change. Through a collaboration with InsuTech companies, they began to examine new ways of providing and promoting insurance services. In a sense, the new tech firms were posing some kind of a threat to the bigger companies by utilizing mobile apps, and customer data analysis. They could disrupt the sector and gain competitive advantages.

Customers showed a marked preference for online interaction to dealing with an agent or broker in person. Apart from this, the other demands from the customers were also increasing. Insurers therefore had to build new products and to adapt to the changed environment.

On-Demand Insurance

It may not be impossible but it is expensive to cover every single thing for all the time. Therefore, a new policy "On-Demand" insurance came into vogue. This is the ability to get insurance coverage whenever one wants and wherever one needs through the use of mobile app. The basic idea was to offer customized insurance with no need to interact with brokers or company representatives.

Many companies now go further and track customer behavior through wearables and get some insight into certain aspects of customer reaction. Further, ML could be used to make some recommendation.

CHAPTER 5

E-Banking

The term "Electronic Banking" (E-banking) could be defined as remote banking services provided by authorized banks or their representatives through devices operated under the bank's direct control and management or under an outsourcing agreement. In other words, E-banking is an umbrella term for the process by which a customer may perform banking transactions electronically without visiting his/her branch and includes the systems that enable customers of such banks to access accounts, transact business, or obtain information on financial products or services through a public or private network.

A remote banking service generally covers under its umbrella the following:

- Dedicated banking service for which the customer has explicitly registered and is so authorized
- Service supplied using devices that are under the control of the provider
- Service which demands the authentication of the customer

E-finance could be used as a generic term to cover banking, insurance, and so on. E-finance very broadly refers to financial services whether delivered online or through other remote mechanisms. They have spread very quickly, almost in all the countries across the globe. There may be differences among countries regarding the readiness and quality of

V. C. Joshi, *Digital Finance, Bits and Bytes*,
https://doi.org/10.1007/978-981-15-3431-7_5

infrastructure. There could even be questions regarding the regulatory norms. But there is considerable commonality and conversion in the spread of E-finance. In this context, it might also be useful to the readers if we define the term "E-money". E-money could broadly be defined as an electronic store of monetary value recorded on a technical device and used for making payments to undertakings other than the issuer without involving bank accounts in the transaction but acting as a pre-paid bearer instrument.

It is customary to classify E-money into following two broad categories:

- Pre-paid stored value cards
- Pre-paid software product that uses computer networks such as Internet

The stored value card uses a microprocessor or chip embedded in a plastic card while software cards need specialized software.

We can now proceed to see the way banks of various hues have responded to the challenges that they had to face in the post crisis period. One has unfortunately to begin with a lack of trust which the customers have in the financial services providers. Curiously enough, banks in particular do not seem to have appreciated the basic need to ensure that customer loyalty to the organization is nurtured at every level. More than anything else it is the trust element that the customers value. We can't forget that like block chains today, double entry book keeping ensured that the trust element that was essential for the fifteenth and sixteenth century traders was enhanced. Banks need clearly to demonstrate that their "policies" are not merely for unhealthy profiteering, and greed for bonuses. The recent example of dishonest practices that were used by Goldman Sachs in case of issuance and distribution of Malaysian bonds are certainly not conducive to trust building. Financial Institutions should be looked up to primarily as honest trustees and custodians. They can't avoid continuous and critical scrutiny because they are dealing with a very sensitive commodity. They must (24/7) be 100% on the correct path and would be judged by standards which are absolute and that need total adherence. Deviations, if any, have to be fully transparent and strictly within given guidelines/rules laid down. Even automated services should be made available only after adequate testing.

We now turn to the emergence of companies who have brought in technology innovations and they are specialists in these fields. We have seen in Chap. 4, that some insurance companies developed what could be described as a completely collaborative approach and brought "Insutech" under the regulatory supervision, guidance, and needs felt by the insurers. This would also ensure that the innovations did meet with the critical regulatory requirements.

In banking, however, quite an opposite trend developed. The FinTechs became attackers on the soft underbelly and the impact was immediately felt on the banks' profits.

We now evaluate the fuller impact of such disruption and the responses of banks and tech companies to this aspect. We begin by bringing out a range of activities and different models that are covered under these broad terms. Broadly, we could classify them as under:

- The first group of companies with somewhat limited capital developed some new products and hesitantly entered the financial services field as competitors. They are willing to be merged with the banks.
- Large technology firms which are already offering directly or indirectly some financial services and can compete very effectively by taking additional activities that enable them to compete effectively with existing players
- Existing competitors who invest on the required scale and therefore tend to be very robust adversaries
- FinTech providers who sell services like the required technology and help managements to digitize

Gradually however, almost 80% of the firms are technology users through any of the means listed above. They had to undergo rigorous testing to meet the requirements of their regulators. Technology used in "developed devices" had to meet rigorous standards laid down by the regulators.

It was not particularly easy to wean bank customers. The customers continuing with their bank for personal/business transactions was rooted in the security aspect. Many a customer have shared their own anxieties when dealing with some unknown entity. The certainty of completion of a given transaction was assured when one dealt with the regulated entity like banks.

The merger with existing institutions was also facilitated to some extent by the FinTech's need for capital, the large customer base of banks, and finally the customer's need for secure execution that could be met under the bank's umbrella.

Disruptive Technology

One has to appreciate the fact that disruption is not a once and for all event. It is an attempt to take over a group of customers with a view to developing relationships over a period of time. The new platforms made the institutions' "Spaghetti Platforms" somewhat inadequate. These came into being because of FIs and Banks adding layers on the existing technology base to meet newer requirements as and when they arose. We would reiterate what disruptive technologies mean. A smaller tech company innovates, brings out a product similar to the one available with FIs and sells it at a price cheaper than that of the FIs. Slowly, it even succeeds in luring upscale customers.

Further these technology changes are not isolated. The proliferation of Internet connections, mobile devices, home computing are all part of the changes that have to be dealt with. These new technologies are putting pressures on traditional business models. The emergence of "Compelling Alternatives" cannot be lightly brushed aside.

Add to it is the fact that the customers have accepted the newer modes of working and are moving away from the bank's distribution avenues. Banks and FIs have to accept the fact that this is not a mere transient phase. New unprecedented threats are looming large. New agile and unregulated entities have come in and threatened traditional players. It needs to be appreciated that the legacy systems, strategies based on them, and the regulations are perhaps preventing the rapid responses the changes warrant.

Banks in particular are faced with two major problems demanding immediate answers. These relate to the way the customers choose to operate their accounts and the products that they need and select. These are interrelated and the answers and dependent action plans cannot be implemented easily.

A survey undertaken by Ernst and Young for the British Banker's Association very clearly shows that the smart mobile phones deliver the convenience the customers desired. 150–180 hits per second was the average use. "Martini Banking" (Martini anywhere/anytime is what the Martini ad said) is what the customers want. They don't like to wait in queues at the counters or at the ATMs. In fact, in some countries like UK, the march toward "cashless" is leading to dismantling of ATM infrastructure and closure of branches. Countries like Spain and Portugal which at one time boasted of their very large branch network are closing these branches. The same trends are becoming visible in India and in other less developed countries. "M-Pesa" is now being shown to have overcome the weaknesses of not having a well-developed financial system.

Banks, as is now clear, have not been able to respond to these changes in ways which appear to be well thought of. Very few banks have taken to establishing stand-alone E-banks or remodeled their branches on the lines of Apple stores. Perhaps the advocates of digital banking would say that banks are miles away from such a course of action. We do however see that newer branch designs meant for serving high net worth individuals to small kiosks are being introduced but have not come into vogue.

Even a quick analysis would show that the transformation cannot take place because of banks' siloed working. Customers do not like to keep on pressing buttons for moving from one department to another or to initiate money transfer. The emergence of mobiles and unprecedented developments on the technology front have given rise to very high expectations for convenience, accessibility, seamless on channel experience, and instant gratification at very low or nil charges. In short, customer's occasional visit to branches would be solely for the purpose for getting advice, or for rectification of errors. It would not be wrong to say that but for a few areas of service, the customers do not want to visit the branches. Only customers who are not very tech-savvy have no option but to use the branch network.

Some bankers have told us that they also detect through faint signals of a reverse trend. They are pointing out to the customers' demand for a human presence in their dealing with the banks or investment advisers. The argument runs somewhat on the lines of what is stated below. A robot adviser would answer a set of questions which a large number of customers ask. These are no doubt satisfactory but do not take care of their peculiar problems like the facilities that one could have after a couple of his/her loans are paid off in a matter of four to six months. Perhaps the particular customer can choose a bigger accommodation in place of the smaller one he is forced to opt for now. Can he get a larger amount at lower rates now since his other liabilities would be reduced? These outwardly appear to be simple queries. For the person concerned and his family members they are very significant. A robot adviser cannot satisfy or remove the anxieties felt by the customer. In the case of the insurance industry, the faster the claim settlement takes place, the greater is the relief for the waiting customers. A similar view was expressed by persons working with the sales department of an airline company.

Banks therefore have to decide on the closure of branches in a satisfactory manner for their millennial customers and at the same time be equally welcoming for the senior citizens or other "thin file" customers. The new digital branches where humans and robots work in close cooperation to fully meet the customer needs is perhaps the answer. The newer designs tailored for high net worth customers at one end to a slightly bigger telephone booth like setup in a rural setting could be the right response. Banks should be aware that merely steam rolling and closing bank's network would not be a right response.

It must be clearly stated more particularly to dispel the impression that banks and insurance companies are passive entities watching and responding to changes in the external environment. Far be from it. They have certain advantages over their competitors and they do and can build on these. Firstly, as regulated institutions with a safety net provided by deposit insurance corporations, banks are able to create a certain degree of assurance in the minds of depositors/investors. It has been amply demonstrated during the 2008–2010 crisis. The fact that the Central Banks' role of being lenders of last resort is a not a mere eyewash. In times of need, the Central Banks do take the required steps and come to the rescue of institutions in difficulties. Secondly, in the post crisis period, the regulators do keep these institutions under a watch and have no hesitation in ring-fencing, stress testing, or in assisting the banks in identifying internal fraudsters as also adopting stern measures whenever necessary. These practices help in creating a safety net around these institutions. Further, the regulators in today's context go all out and undertake critical evaluation of new technical products before being deployed in the work environment. The competitors (GAFA excluded) suffer from not having a customer base and adequate capital resources to grow. Figure 5.1 compares and contrasts FIs and FinTechs.

Apart from the defenses indicated above, banks have other means of competing. They have a treasure trove in the form of information about their customers and their needs. They can easily come out (using these resources) with suitable and desirable products. One such instance vividly stands out. J. P. Morgan have setup a subsidiary unit for such an analytical work. They undertook a study covering some millions of customers to assess the impact of fluctuations in income over a period of time. They are

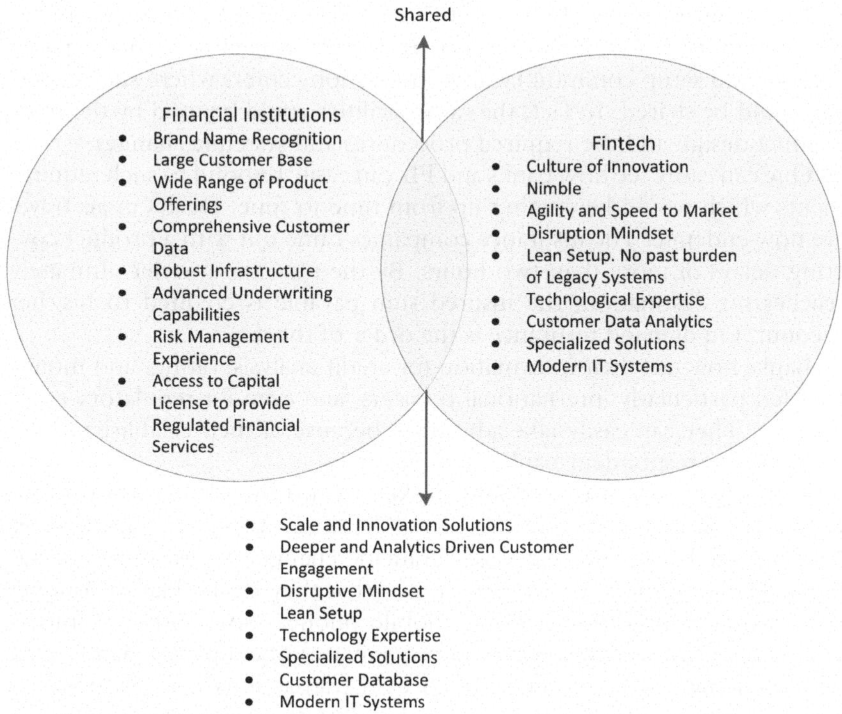

Fig. 5.1 Disruptive technologies. (Source: World Economic Forum)

now able to design and offer suitable products to tide over the problems of such customers.

True it is, that data analysts are a rare commodity and that their salaries in the USA are going up by about 16% every year. But even a crude review of recruitment suggests that Wall Street or finance companies in California are not finding it too difficult to recruit talented staff. Further, even contract appointments with finance companies are sought after. Compared to FinTechs, FIs are in a better position to hire analysts, consultants, and even appointees on contract.

Coming now to Artificial Intelligence (AI), between 2014 and 2016, nearly 216 algorithms were developed for and by the finance companies. The simplification of procedures, automation of activities by Financial Institutions is where these algorithms are being used. The collaboration of

FIs with management schools is far easier today and others find it difficult to compete with FIs in this respect. In less developed countries, smaller banks could setup common facility/innovation centers where such expertise could be shared. In fact, the same facilities could be used by them for product design and the required procedures and systemic changes.

One can easily see how banks and FIs can easily respond to such requirements which would be coming up from time to time. Delays in air travel are now endemic. The insurance companies came out with a product covering delays of more than two hours. By the time the traveler ultimately reaches his destination, the insured sum payable is credited to his/her account. On demand insurance is the order of the day.

Banks now use their information for credit analysis, rating, and money transfer, particularly international transfers, and even for regulatory compliances. They can easily take advantage because of their established connections (correspondent banks) and channels.

The playing field was no doubt stacked against the FIs but it was by no means beyond them to tide over the difficulties. A bigger challenge was awaiting the banks and that was a dramatic change in customer expectations. The customers have clearly shown that they would like to conduct their transactions through smart mobile phones. Soon other countries could come to this cashless state is not a matter of conjecture any longer. The avoidance of a tax net through cash transactions may disappear as cashless would be the order of the day. But the information collected through various sources could be put to use to build a rapport with the customers. In the first place, avoid duplication of work. A very simple case would bring home this point. In case a person's salary were credited to his/her account monthly/fortnightly, why ask for a salary slip if and when required. The bank already has this information. These days even dividend income gets credited to one's designated account.

As unofficial investment advisers the banks could certainly bring to a client's notice, the rock bottom balance in his account and suggest that the client postpone a given purchase or if required, arrange for an overdraft facility.

The data from wearables is making it quite easy. A toothbrush company is reported to have indicated to some users the need for an appointment with the dentist. This may sound too intrusive but in case of the bank could be seen as a watchful hint from the guardian of your resources.

Inclusive Banking

We now turn to a very important question facing the banks. The "thin file" customers were invariably excluded from the purview of banks/FIs. The time has now come for the banks to give up this hands-off approach and add this very large segment to their customer net. Perhaps they ought to review their business model in toto and turn themselves into a common man's bank. We have met with very stiff resistance for this suggestion. The first and most obvious is the cost of the transaction argument. It is no longer valid. Mobile technology has brought down the cost per transaction. The only cost could be fixed cost to be spread or distributed over various activities and technology maintenance and depreciation costs.

This brings us to our major suggestion. In most countries particularly less developed ones, the banks have avoided lending directly to such customers. They were left to fend for themselves. The space thus left open by banks was taken up by Microfinance Institutions (MFIs)/and NGOs who borrowed money from the banks and lent it to the poverty-stricken clients. Equally important, the private money lenders or local traders also lent money. They would borrow from the banks and do it. In most of the cases, exorbitant interest was charged and recovered. In some cases, there was a group guarantee scheme also in operation. In case of default, the members of the group would go to any length to coerce the defaulting ones. Frankly, the means used to recover such loans under the guarantee scheme are abhorring.

In addition, this whole model suffers from a fundamental weakness. The assumption underlying the small loan scheme is that the poorer sections can start business activity and easily turn themselves into entrepreneurs. This may be a perfect fit in a liberal ideology but in practice it is nothing but a myth perpetuated. A Nigerian woman turning herself into a sheep farmer and offering jobs to one or two other women is probably a rare example. Surveys have brought out that most of the people hanker for jobs with secure monthly income and aspire to get Government jobs. There is another drawback. The banks had to bear all the losses whenever defaults took place. The MFIs could not or did not repay the loans whenever there was a crisis. This was vividly brought out in India during the Andhra Pradesh crisis of 2011. Secondly, while the default risks are borne by banks, the benefits were reaped by the MFIs. All this rigmarole of lending to MFIs was for the banks to show to the regulators and the owners that they did finance the poorer sections.

The banks however need not follow this path. They have a number of other options like

- Treat these loans as consumption loans. They could in fact help the poorer sections in acquiring things at reasonable rates. The poorer people should not be at the mercy of traders, that is close the information asymmetry.
- Work out recovery packages after taking a note of the various circumstances in which the borrower finds himself or herself. Most of these loans can be recovered if a careful analysis of the borrower's economic condition is undertaken. We have noted that in Vietnam, in case of families who have to take care of one or two war veterans, due allowances are made by the recovery agents who are associated with the loan process right from the beginning.

Banks must not cover their not undertaking these activities by transferring them to the NGOs and treating them for a much bigger noble purpose like women empowerment. We would go a step further and say that banks must coordinate with the Government's welfare activities and/or undertake schemes which would benefit a wider group and also help in promoting participation by the whole group.

Very often we are asked about the financing of such activities and the costs for money lodged. We would certainly recommend that banks must use innovative products like Social Impact Bonds. The banks have to take a clear and unequivocal stance and not try to perpetuate a myth. Opening this as an important channel in their business model must be done with a clear understanding. Banks should undertake this as a business venture and not as a social charity.

We would conclude this section by saying that technology for the first time opens up a new business channel and banks can very easily harness newer technology and take full advantage of it. The field is as open to them as one would wish to. They need not depend on the crutches of the intermediaries. Digital lending, risk modelling, mobile operations, and E-insurance have altered the scene. It is the will that is lacking now.

We now turn to another area which is a must in today's technology context. It is supplemental and a must for the activities proposed in the paragraphs above. The training/education for financial literacy would be the cornerstone of the banks' functioning. Banks have to give up the idea that a vast majority of their poorer customers would never be able to use and harness this technology in their day to day life. Technology can be properly made use of when and only when it becomes accessible to most of the customers. A drive in this behalf in a sustained manner is called for. Dummy branches where customers get to know the rudiments and acquire the necessary skills is a must. Further the technology should be used by the weaker segments of their customers with a clear understanding that

- Any haphazard way may land them in difficulties
- These are only different ways for making an intelligent use of their funds
- There are a number of ways in which to meet their urgent financial needs through careful and judicious planning.

There are innumerable teaching methods available starting with animation and ending with hands on experience at dummy branches. Banks must realize that this activity is foundational and required to be undertaken beyond banking hours. The customer's convenience is of paramount importance.

Open Banking Movement

It is in a sense a response to the customer's changing requirements that the banks are expected to share data and afford access to consumers and small account holders through a common framework of application programming. It would in all likelihood fuel a wave of innovation and also bring about a level playing field. It does afford an opportunity for FinTechs seeking entry through payments/consumer finance etc. The EU payment service directive updates and enhances the EU rules in place. PSD2 came into force from 12th January 2016 and members had time till January 2018 to transport it into national law. The main objectives of PSD2 are as follows.

1. To contribute to a more integrated and efficient European payments market.
2. To further level the playing field for payment services provider by including new players
3. To make payments safer and more secure
4. To enhance protection for European consumers and businesses

In other words, PSD2 supports innovation and competition in retail payments and enhances the security of payment transactions and also affords protection to consumers for their data. It must be noted that PSD2 is supplemented by regulatory technical standards on customer authentication and common and secure open standard as well as guidelines.

The regulatory technical standards include

- Allowing for authorization
- To dynamically link specific amount and payee
- Offering of transactions and device monitoring to understand unusual payment patterns
- Provision of a standard and reliable access interface to payment accounts

The other key change introduced by PSD2 can be grouped into four main but overlapping themes.

- Market efficiency and integration
- Consumer protection
- Competition
- Choice and Security

Some other changes include

- Extension of scope to all currencies and one leg payment transaction
- Passporting authorization rules and supervision of payments by institutions
- Consumer Protection
- New Providers and New Payment Service
- Operational and Security Risk Management and Incident Reporting
- Requirements for a strong customer authentication and secure communication

Customers will have the option to share information about how they operate the account with organizations that would work to deliver and enhance banking experience by offering comparisons and switching services to help customers in identifying the best product.

The UK authorities, who have already passed similar regulations, expect a clear statement from banks regarding the persons to whom such facilities and services would be made available It is clear that such changes would open up new markets and encourage new entrants and even to those who were excluded.

It would also enable customers to shop online without the need for payment cards. Such payments could be initiated directly from their bank account. Customers would be provided with a consolidated view of the accounts held by them with various banks. The customers will have the possibility of analyzing their financial data and examine the affordability and availability of cheap finance. Lastly, they would be able to see where they could get cheap credit and avail of cheap services required.

Internet Banking

There are two types of Internet Banks which are referred to as stand-alone banks, and as the name suggests, operate almost exclusively on the Internet. Accounts are opened and transactions are conducted during stipulated business hours. Non-Internet communications are kept to the minimum.

The banks which are also known as "Cyber-Banks" are online operations of existing banks and/or building societies. These banks offer online access. They offer competitive rates and options, all the while making banking more convenient. Among the names which crop up are

1. Federal Revenue Department on Consumer and Mobile banking
2. Synchrony bank
3. CIT bank
4. Dime Community Banks
5. Capital One 360 etc.

The reasons they attract consumers can be summed up as under:

- Convenient
- Lower fees

They are found to be highly competitive. They do have FDIC protection. But many of them do not have debt focused products. They have numerous ways of making deposits. Customers can make payments on line. Paper checks are deposited on line. It is as simple as mapping a picture of the front and back of the check. Further electronic fund transfers are also permitted.

There are many reasons for a switch. But the main one is that the costs are up to 400 times lower than traditional channels. The branch costs add to total costs almost 400 basis point. It does allow a facility to transfer surplus cash from the branch account and earn higher interest from the Internet branch and, bring back the cash, if and when required.

Stand Alone E-Banks

We give below a detailed review of a Bank in Poland to show how such a bank functions as a stand-alone bank. Alior Bank is a fully virtual bank. It works 24 hours a day, 7 days a week on-line with a variety of contact options including video conversations and advice. The customers can buy products and request consultants to complete forms for them. The forms are displayed on the screen so that the customer can see the progress.

Apple and Google like stores provide full accessibility and integration through smart phones and other devices. One could have:

- Checking and Savings and transfer money if required
- Bank status
- Quick Domestic Transfers via mobile
- Facebook [social networks in general]
- Money transfer with a camera on mobile of an invoice
- Entertainment zone offers, tickets for music concerts etc. With discounts/or zero percent plans
- Bank can easily bring in mobile personalization and virtualization and improve on its customer services with deep data mining.

To sum up, we could say that they have all the elements of new mobile and Internet banking applications. To name a few, they have video verification for customer over boarding, proactive approach to PSD2-Open Ap banking, partnerships with FinTechs. The digitized lending process is there. In short it is equipped with all the latest amenities which a digital bank would aspire to have.

We would, however, like to particularly highlight the way their research center works.

All lab members continuously work on identifying disruptive ideas. They concentrate on R&D, ways of cooperating with FinTechs, the viability of disruptive ideas is examined. And the whole organization is involved in such creative thinking. It is, no doubt, a demanding work. They have to be up-to-date with new trends, market trends, market changes, and new technologies. The Director of research very aptly sums up their approach. "What is at issue is to easily forget what we learnt yesterday and quickly absorb new approaches to every performed task. While innovating we should be able to bring together things that won't go together and look critically at projects worked out earlier. You would not get new results using old methods."

Digital Banking

Since 2014 or thereabouts analysts have been advocating radical transformation of banking as was practiced a few years earlier. Their analysis begins with a review of the major forces shaping the banking business map.

On the one hand we have customers who are technically savvy and rarely use the branch network. They are not loyal to a given institution and if they do happen to have a somewhat long-term relationship, they would expect to be suitably rewarded for such a long-term association. The younger set [digital natives] would be quite content to carry the bank in their pockets. They are quite content with their mobiles meeting all their needs.

Equally important are the developments on the technology front. And developments like open banking would be the features they would be hankering for. They are not likely to have [unlike their elderly relations] any affinity for branch banking. Alternately some of them describe these as meeting places for the elderly.

It is natural that authors like Skinner [Digital Banking] are proposing a thorough overhaul starting with branch architecture and design (even electrical wiring to suit the newer technology) applications. In terms of work systems the current compartmentalized working would be done away with and new groupings would be determined by customer preferences as shown by their transactions undertaken and preferences as shown by data analysis.

The centers would be redesigned more like Apple stores and would have robots and a few banking/investment experts on call to meet the customer by prior appointment. It would be the banks' endeavor to see that a symbiotic relationship develops between the robots and humans working there. These designs would be tailored in different ways and would range from luxurious settings for high net worth customers to telephone booths like but more spacious for rural areas. Such designs are available and we give below the links for the readers to get an idea of what it would be like. In times of difficult natural conditions the staff could be on call to guide the customers and in normal time it could well be a place for socializing and meeting different customer segments.

Frankly it is all in the realm of possibility. How soon it gets translated into action is the question. True it is that time-poor customers would like such fast dispensation of services. They need not wait in queues and would avoid being directed from desk to desk. They would also not like to keep on pressing buttons to move from department to department. The service has to be seamless. The elderly would see their branch being closed and would not have the luxury of cash being handed over to them as they are busy collecting the local gossip!

The difficulties in digitization are stupendous. Costs for dismantling the legacy systems, terminating the jobs of low skilled employees would pose problems on a scale not encountered before. The journey ahead is going to be extremely difficult and turbulent. Changing existing systems, and adopting all practices to be in sync with the digital working requirements is by no means an easy task. Additionally, there would be problems of merged entities being properly enmeshed into the banks' culture. Some time would have to elapse to reach the digital Nirvana.

CHAPTER 6

E-Trading

In this chapter we are restricting ourselves to an analysis primarily of securities trading. We would primarily cover trading in shares, and government paper, or treasuries, as it is commonly denominated.

We would begin with an observation that our previous conclusions which showed that there was enough scope for brick and click to coexist and that investment decisions would demand a strong hand holding element and that brokers and bankers would certainly retain their prime position as dispensers of securities could not stand the test of time. Subsequent actions of the investors have proved us to be completely wrong. The investor behavior, has, brought out a pattern which is at variance with what we had suggested might happen. It was not envisaged that the advice coming from a robot on the pick of instruments for investment would become acceptable. It is proved that artificial intelligence does afford solutions which are superior to the ones selected by humans. Studies at MIT have conclusively brought out the superiority of such techniques and the brokers and their research advisors have a comparatively diminished role in predicting risk profiles or even the choice of portfolios based on the analysis. The downward spiral of commissions and the emergence of high frequency trading with its "dark pool" are clear indications that the time-tested brokering practice is on the wane.

The term, "Electronic Trading", or E-Trading, encompasses a wide variety of trading systems ranging from simple order transmission services to full-fledged trade-execution facilities. It is therefore useful to define

V. C. Joshi, *Digital Finance, Bits and Bytes*,
https://doi.org/10.1007/978-981-15-3431-7_6

E-Trading in a somewhat broader context. It is a facility that provides some or all of the following services:

- Electronic order routing from users to the system
- Automated trade execution—translating orders into trade
- Electronic dissemination of bid/offer quotes and depth
- Post trade information

It is necessary to cover in this definition even those systems, which do not include trade execution facilities. The purpose here is not to examine the system but to look at E-Trading in general and its impact.

Compared to the earlier systems, E-Trading has certain advantages and those need to be highlighted. The use of computers and mobile devices automate aspects of trading process and changes the relationship amongst dealers and customers. It is not merely building a better smart phone, but to create a new way of trading differently from either floor trading or through smart phones. We would particularly highlight the following differences:

- E-Trading is location neutral
- It allows multilateral interaction
- E-Trading is scalable. Such systems are/can be scaled up to handle more trade by simply increasing the capacity of the computer network. The scalability can enhance the reach of the dealers through a greater access to a widening base.
- Operational costs under the E-Trading system can be reduced because economies of scale can be exploited.
- E-Trading system is integrated. It allows straight-through processing by integrating different parts of the trading.

The casualty is the intermediary. The brokerage houses and their role as intermediaries have undergone a change.

This brings us to the uses of the mobile devices for trading; sometime back the Mumbai stock exchange launched its MobiTrack service which allows the user to access stock price details such as last traded price, percentage change in each scrip and also profile of few scrips selected by the user. It must be mentioned that the risks as in the case of banks would be there. Even systemic risks would be very much there. Steps can be taken to guard against breaches or misuse of the system.

Before proceeding to the question of the role of intermediaries we would discuss the present high frequency trading practices. Today's trading is lot more complex and involves little human intervention. Most importantly trading is done in microseconds or less— less than a blink of an eye. The availability of a number of platforms along with significant technological advancements makes the process, by which orders are routed and executed, highly complex. Broker dealers use digital algorithms to route different portions of an order to different venues in various sequences, taking into account the many factors, such as, minimization of market impact, minimization of information leakage, immediacy, and cost of execution.

High Frequency Trading

The high frequency trading (HFT) is an authorized way for executing transactions through an exchange. The broad characteristics of such high frequency trading can be briefly summed up as under:

- Use of extraordinarily high-speed programs for generating, routing, and executing orders.
- Use of collocation services and individual data feed offered by exchanges to minimize network, and other types of latencies (Collocation to market is an arrangement with trading centers to rent space to market participants so that these participants can locate their servers in close proximity to a trading center's matching engine)
- Short time for establishing and liquidating positions
- Numerous orders can be submitted and executed in short time frame
- End the day with flat positions

We would, along with such HFT practices, also mention the existence of "dark pools". These pools, as it is sometimes claimed, allow traders to hide their activities from regulators. However, a perusal of the reports from Securities and Exchange Commission (SEC), Commodities Future Trading Commission, and Financial Industry Regulatory Authority shows that they are able to monitor transactions within such pools and can initiate action when warranted.

In a sense dark pools are a form of alternate trading systems, which means they are regulated as broker-dealer rather than an exchange. Prices are not disclosed to other traders but are matched anonymously

Table 6.1 Advantages and disadvantages of HFT

Advantages	*Disadvantages*
Increased liquidity	Liquidly is phantom and not real
Lower market volatility	Exacerbates market fragility
Reduced bid/ask spreads and lower	Increases market systemic risks
Better price discovery	Certain strategies amount to manipulation
Generally proprietary trading	Two tier market System
Reduced executive time	
Better price discovery	

Source: PWC—An objective look at high-frequency trading and dark pool. http://313ct818yszd3xd6xa2z47nm-wpengine.netdna-ssl.com/wp-content/uploads/2015/07/pwc-high-frequency-trading-dark-pools.pdf

against contra side orders. Once trades are executed, they are transferred and reported immediately to the consolidated tape and become known. We summarize the advantages and disadvantages of the HFT in Table 6.1.

Add to this, the Front Running—defined as using the knowledge of an incoming order to take a favorable position in the market. The SEC had sought the opinions of researchers and others on certain aspects of trading activities and tried to evaluate the impact, both positive and negative, of such HFT activities. Their conclusions are, no doubt tentative, but anyone familiar with working with stock market data sets would appreciate the difficulties inherent to such studies.

SEC had sought the opinions on the following four aspects:

- Passive Market Making
- Arbitrage
- Structural problems
- Directional situations

Passive Market Making

It involves the submission of non-marketable resting orders that provide liquidity to the market at specified prices. These passive orders are not executed immediately but have to rest on the order book. Their prices need to be updated frequently to reflect changing market conditions. This naturally results in an enormous number of order cancellations or modifications.

Arbitrage strategy generally seeks to capture pricing disparities between related products or markets, such as, Exchange Traded products and its underlying basket of stocks. Arbitrage strategies do not depend on directional moves but rather on price convergence.

Normally directional strategies involve establishing a long or short position in anticipation of a price move upward or downward. The SEC wanted to assess the possibilities arising from order anticipation that may pose particular problems for long-term investors. Order anticipation seeks to ascertain the existence of large buyers/sellers in the market place and then trade ahead of those buyers in anticipation that their orders will move the markets.

A momentum ignition strategy involves anticipating a series of orders and trades to ignite a rapid move up or down. This kind of trading practice is not proper but it is true that technology can allow proprietary firms to better identify and execute such strategies.

There is a feeling that HFT firms may employ aggressive anticipation and momentum strategies and such strategies may worsen transaction costs for institutional investors, and may contribute to market volatility.

We must take note of competition amongst HFTs. Competition may increase intraday volatility and reduce liquidity but has no effect on intraday volatility.

A review by SEC of HFT working during "Flash Crash" shows that HFTs did not trigger the flash crash but their response to the unusually large selling pressure exacerbated market volatility.

E-Trading in Government Securities and Fixed Income Securities

Since 1990, starting with treasuries, the most liquid securities, trading began in these instruments and currently is quite a dominant part of the market products. Equally worth noting is the development in trading of other less liquid fixed income securities also. Corporate bonds and Municipal bonds also form a significant portion of the marketed instruments. It is worth mentioning that there are about 130 trading platforms for Municipal bonds in USA.

Immediately after the 2008 crisis, banks had liquidity and capital adequacy problems and were somewhat restricted in their trading activities. But this helped in opening up trading platforms for Municipal bonds etc. Since 2012 open trading platforms became available, and bond traders could trade without brokers. Many broker/dealers have now shifted to Municipal bonds/high yield corporate bonds.

It is worth noting that while trading in corporate shares etc. has declined there is an increase in the number of trades in the fixed income category. With the emergence of E-Trading considerable improvements have taken place and some governments (notably in India) permit individuals to buy treasuries in smaller lots from their bankers. We list below some of the advantages emanating from the availability of E-Trading facility.

- Improved Liquidity—Investors can now submit a request for quotation [RFQ] to receive an immediate bid/offer from investment managers, broker/dealers, or even banks
- Platforms provide recent history
- Trading takes place within seconds—Faster trading reduces the risk of news regarding interest rates filtering through
- Reduced Charges—Platforms generally charge very nominally as a mark up to the price

One precautionary note:

It is absolutely necessary to quote the correct price, size and precisely correct bonds required. Mistakes could be very costly and could exacerbate liquidity problems. Mistakes on this score are quite numerous. The monetary losses incurred can cause a very heavy burden.

We have deliberately refrained from dealing with problems of market structures for the bond market. We find that these are pretty well defined and documented in simple to understand language. To quote one example the Reserve Bank of India has published hand books giving detailed information and FAQs. Anyone can glean the required particulars.

We now turn to the Regulatory Issues. It is increasingly becoming difficult for regulators to keep pace with technological developments, corporate arrangements—a change from mutualization to limited liabilities of the dealers and exchanges for various alternate trading systems now available. We, therefore, turn to the analytical framework and assumptions on which the regulatory system functions and tries to keep pace with the changing ecosystem. The main question that comes up is: Is it better to continue to add to the existing statutes or should a new approach be adopted? In a speech on this subject, delivered at Harvard, in July 2017, we came across a reference to a paper on scientific revolution by Thomas S. Kuhn in his study of "The Structures of Scientific Revolution." Kuhn argues that science does not develop in linear progression with one discovery leading logically to the next. The normal inquiry proceeds under the widely accepted rules. Scientists obtain results which do not comport with the predictions anticipated under a given paradigm. The discord between the predicated and actual results leads to a crisis. Thereafter assumptions under the paradigm are challenged, questioned, and deconstructed. The idea was to support the argument that such changes are slow and that they come after the old ones are tried and shown to be not effective. The old and the new paradigm coexist. It continues till the new paradigm is accepted. Initially securities trading was regulated by federal laws and the paradigm within that framework. A similar trend is noticeable in the case of Regulatory measures. Certain rules/laws are passed and implemented. Later on the market situation changes and the laws seem to have become redundant. New rules become necessary. New acts are passed. This is what happened in case of regulations brought in by the New Deal legislation that followed the 1929 stock market crash.

Between 1933 and 1940 as many as six statutes were adopted. But basically, the basis was one of self-regulation. The brokers and exchanges were left to regulate their own working. It was observed that over a period of time it became difficult for the members to control their business practices and exercise the required supervisory functions. Amongst the undesirable practices noticed one could mention the following:

- Manipulative Stock Pools
- Insider Trading
- Offering profitable securities to preferred lists
- Avoiding Federal prohibition on securities by operating state-chartered securities firms etc.

It then brought to the fore important questions—Should economic incentives or ethics and responsibilities control the operations of the capital markets? A number of statutes were passed and regulatory rule making had to be resorted to. The "Micro Intervention Paradigm" became the order of the day. The Securities Act, the Exchange Act, the Public Utility Company's Holding Act and many other acts were brought in. The New Deal built laws which necessitated mandatory registration and called for transparency. Accountants and lawyers were brought in to ensure proper registration. Industry professionals would look at the business aspects and to remove glitches, if any. Over-the-counter activities were regulated through an Association. These self-policing organizations would supervise their members and take disciplinary actions when required. This was termed as "Cooperative Regulation" in which jobs were done by investment bankers, brokers, dealers, with the government "exercising dual control." Apart from supporting the members' interests the association was expected to regulate the members' behavior through continuous program of rulemaking, interpretation, surveillance, and enforcement of the applicable federal securities laws and its own ethical standards. The Exchange act and the Maloney act completed the paradigm of an integrated system of regulation managed in the first instance by market professionals.

The system continued for nearly 35 years. But the sheer volume of transactions (came to be known as a paper crisis) i.e. the volume of traded securities skyrocketed but the industry did not modernize the system. Reducing working hours, stopping business on Wednesdays could not solve the problem. The Association was too slow in grasping the problem and sought authority in:

- Processing of securities transactions
- The rule making authority
- Enforcement SRO Rules
- Administration of disciplinary proceedings
- Development of an automated system

The idea was to build a system which was:

- Economically Efficient
- Fair Competition amongst players
- Information Availability
- Practicality of Order Fulfillment
- Customer Orders to be completed without brokers—the commission to implement

A new paradigm is coming into being. It incorporates elements of self-regulatory structure and seeks to make it more effective by allowing the commission to influence or impose the structures on the Industry.

The commission thus gets drawn into addressing the mechanics of equity market structures on a regular and active basis. New technologies, new models, and new instruments taxed the existing concepts and regulations requiring an ever-increasing guidance, interpretation, and rule-making.

The problem to be solved was that the National Association of Securities Dealers lacked the internal controls necessary to manage the conflict between responsibilities to oversee the brokers and its operations of the market. The commission worked on the structural aspects of the market but the policies of the SROs continued to pose problems. There is a need to see that both the sides are balanced.

Basically, the commission has to determine the proper ways for routing the broker/dealer orders, routing orders and prices charged for access to quotations. The problem today is to see if it makes sense now or is it better to leave it to the market?

On an, as is where is basis, there are a number of authorities to control these institutions, such as, Comptroller of Currency, Commodity Futures Trading Commissioner, Consumer Financial Protection Bureau. Each of these has a different mandate and in some cases their jurisdictions overlap. Naturally there are turf wars over jurisdictional issues, and the institutions would be faced with cross-firing dilemmas.

Basically, the question before the Regulatory Commission is at an inflection point. There is a conflict about micro level intervention and leaving it to the market approach. On the one hand there is a view that the US equity markets are most liquid, transparent, efficient, and competitive in the world. Spreads have declined and so have transaction costs.

But curiously the general perception is that they are not fair. The system withstood the "Flash Crash" of 2010. But for the public it was not a price adjustment mechanism but the equity market turned into a casino. The traders who possess an informational advantage exploit it for their own benefit. Thus, fairness is the reason for regulation.

The regulators have two issues to decide on. Should they leave the system and the players to regulate themselves? They know the problems and while individuals may to an extent be swayed by "biases" institutions are less likely to be swayed by it. One then comes to the conclusion that rule making only spirals into more and more rules and autonomy could to an extent result in certain compromise, one could leave it to the players and hope that symbiotic relationship could develop. Our own experience of the working of a regional stock exchange shows that it is extremely difficult for the Boards, and members of the regulatory committee to do the policing required. Self-regulation has serious limitations. Outside members [independent directors on the Board of the Exchange] cannot do much to impose rules strictly. In varying degrees members of the governing body are also involved in some such practice sought to be controlled.

On the other hand, are consumer protectionists and regulators who use numerous techniques to see if there is an attempt to use consumer biases, behavioral weaknesses and other drawbacks that are being used for misleading the consumers in buying the financial products. They are using big data, advanced mathematical tools, inputs from neuro sciences, machine learning, and behavioral analytics to draw their inferences and then use regulatory processes to rectify the wrongs. These measures also imply bringing in some ethical considerations. Currently Australia and UK are using behavioral tools to reform their regulatory systems and one would have to see how effective these measures are.

In this situation, one is driven to conclude that it would be best to leave the system untouched and allow it to evolve, as if by a natural process. We tend to agree with a commissioner of securities commission who in a talk at Harvard seemed to suggest that ultimately, we would have to allow the system to develop a symbiotic relationship and evolve practices which would be for the good of the system. In a very apt illustration, he quotes the example of corals which change their color at night and during the day to suit the needs of the algae that survives essentially through this change process. One need not assume that mere self-interest would, even at the cost of serious consequences for the system would prevail and everything else would be thrown to the wind. After all, the rogue traders are few. At the moment to allow sense to prevail seems to be the best policy.

Foreign Exchange (ForEx) Trading

In the early 1980s electronic trading platforms were installed by stock exchanges and were found quite useful by the clients. However, for the forex markets they were not adequate. In fact, they were "slow" and did not meet the trader's needs. They could not settle "trades" in real time.

The last few years could be considered as periods of major changes. It has availability (access at any time) in mobile trading. Coupled with these were changes in algorithm and gradual elimination of human intervention. The emergence of High Frequency computers through which high volume of trades are executed. Naturally, the time taken for settlement is in seconds.

It is true that programmed trading aggravates the problems as was seen during crisis periods. One would need to be vigilant to detect early signs of pressures building up. Further major banks can try and do get certain advantages denied to smaller players.

One wonders if the "Libor" manipulation was a response by the traders to machine trading over which they had no control. Automatic trading robots signal to guide users. Robots removed the need for the traders' intervention. The latest would be having robots to deal for you.

The Libor Manipulation

It is against this background that we need to view the Libor Manipulations. Unfortunately, even Senior Bank management connive at the very bad practices being used by dealers.

The London interbank offered rate scandal was discovered and it came to light that the banks were falsely inflating or deflating their rates so as to profit from trades or to give the impression that they truly prevented the banks' needs for short-term lending/borrowing. There were a number of fraudulent transactions and even manipulations once the fraud became known, E-mails, record of phone calls and so on became available and brought out how pervasive the scandal had become.

The British Government appointed committee and it is now decided that "Libor" would not be operative from 2021. In the USA alternative arrangements are being put in place. It is going to be somewhat time consuming as Libor was a reference rate in many contracts. It does seem that greed takes over and systems suffer losses not thought of. The regulatory balance is delicate and it is for the players to ensure its stability.

Both the securities trading and Forex trading are fraud prone areas. Frauds of one sort or the other are endemic to these activities and very important regulatory and supervisory issues come up.

In both these cases self-regulatory approach does not seem to have succeeded in catching it. In the USA, the S.E.C. has clearly admitted that SROs are not able to effectively handle the various questions. In fact, when there were paper operations the regulatory system broke down under the “paper” volumes. In the case of “Libor”, the larger banks and their trades were themselves the perpetrators.

We are led to conclude that in the light of this colossal failure, there is a need for strict regulatory and supervisory overview. The regulators need to be vigilant not only about the reported trades but also about front running and dark pools, products sold and even the technology used.

CHAPTER 7

Cyber-Crimes and -Laws

If the cyber-space is a community, a giant neighborhood made up of networked computer users around the world, then it seems natural that many elements of a traditional society can be found taking shape as bits and bytes. Cyber-crime can be defined as the occurrence of one or the combination of the following events in a computer environment. The events are unauthorized attempts to access, alter, add, delete, or hide the data or the defined systems, stealing of data or programs in any manner, and unauthorized entry into the computer environment. Cyber-space is a virtual tourist spot where faceless, nameless con artists can work the crowds. Still more sinister are the well-organized perpetrators of such crimes and sometimes even states are reported to be involved in such activities. Computer criminals comprise co-workers, insiders, disgruntled employees, or even those who do it for fun, competitors and others. We have in the Chap. 9 on managing Cyber-risks dealt with the way these elements commit such crimes or contribute to perpetrating such crimes or are actively involved in them.

A distinct shift in criminal activities is noticeable in the way such crimes are committed. Increasingly, criminals are finding that there is no need to take the risk that gangs/robbers take. Instead of digging tunnels and breaking open the banks' vaults, they could make more money by using just a keyboard and a dongle. Apart from the fact they don't have to worry about hidden CCTV cameras, they have a comparatively simple task of breaching a firewall. There is a perception that it is unlikely that the

V. C. Joshi, *Digital Finance, Bits and Bytes*,
https://doi.org/10.1007/978-981-15-3431-7_7

criminals would be caught or even when they commit a crime. Further, in spite of their loot, the punishment that they are likely to get would not be what it would be, if they were caught robbing the bank.

We have briefly described the sectors which are subjected to the cyber-attacks and the losses suffered by institutions. Crime is any activity that is a legal wrong that can be followed by criminal proceedings which may result in punishment. Lord Atkin very succinctly describes it as: "The criminal quality of an act cannot be discovered by reference to any standard but one: Is the Act prohibited with penal consequences?" Cyber-crime may be said to be those species of which the genus is the conventional crime, and where either the computer is an object or subject for the conduct constituting crime. Any unauthorized attempt to access, modify, add, delete, or hide the data in any manner comes under the cyber-crime category.

Why do these crimes occur? The perceived anonymity and the huge financial gains could be the main reasons. Coming down to more specific reasons one could list the following:

- Research and Development expenses for a competitor who steals the information, would be nil and would allow the competitor to go ahead in technology
- Network Administrator's laxity
- The networked systems and crimes often go undetected
- Disgruntled employees could try to breach the systems
- Misuse of social engineering sites for gaining access

The ease with which a crime can be committed turns out to be a provocation for such temptation.

- Cryptographic keys can be figured out by timing the computers
- Firewalls and system probing are easier than digging tunnel to the 'bank's vault
- Password Cracker Programs try every word in the dictionary as a password
- Network files to share data between systems is exploited through well-known vulnerabilities
- Network "sniffing" collects authorized passwords by monitoring data traffic

- Viruses are transmitted through documents that are attached to Emails and are activated when documents are opened

For the sake of illustrating our earlier statement about the laws prescribing penalties for certain action we would refer the reader to sections 43[a], 43[b], of the Information Technology Act 2000 as amended in 2012. It should be borne in mind that any person who helps another person

- to gain unauthorized access
- to damage a computer
- to manipulate data for financial benefit
- to transfer the service charges to an account of a person who has not availed of the service

We refer to and draw on the Indian information Act as the same is based on UNCITRAL model law framework and would have applicability generally. Table 7.1 lists the nature of several crimes and their impacts.

Table 7.1 Cyber-crimes and their effects

Criminal Act	*Possible manifestation*	*Potential effect*
Unauthorized system access	Hacker enters internal systems, confidential information is intercepted, data corrupted, crash of system	Loss of data, Unauthorized copying of information/data, repairing perceived insecurity of system
Employee fraud	Alteration of data to draw funds from accounts, card fraud	Reimbursement of customer losses in accordance with RBI guide lines, reconstruction of accurate data, sanctions/regulatory sanctions In accordance with RBI Guidelines (Limited liability of customer)
Counterfeiting of electronic money	Criminals alter or duplicate electronic money to obtain goods or funds	Liability for falsified money. Replacing costs associated with a compromised system
Repudiation of a transaction	Customer denial for a completed transaction	Possible loss of funds or legal expenses to prove otherwise
Significant breach of security	Introduction of virus	Loss of customers/other may follow
Money laundering	Misuse by criminals	Legal sanction for noncompliance

Source: *BIS*—Risk management measures in retail electronic banking and electronic money. https://www.bis.org/publ/bcbs35.pdf

Lalita Shridhar, a noted jurist, has rightly pointed out that our understanding of the virtual world is woefully slim; and of cyber-crimes even less. But their effect on the real world is devastating. The term cyber denotes virtual space and it means informational space modeled through a computer, in which various objects and symbol images of information exist. It is the place where computer programs work and data is processed. The term crime refers to social and economic phenomenon as old as the human society. Crime is a legal concept and has punishment under law. Crime is a legal wrong that can be followed by criminal proceedings which may result into punishment. The most important criminal quality of an act is the breach of criminal law. We could well say that cyber-crime is an act where a computer is either a tool or target or both. These crimes can be committed against an individual, against organizations, against government, and against society at large. Such crimes also include the following:

- Harassment via E-mails
- Cyber-Stalking
- Dissemination of obscene material
- Defamation
- E-Mail Spoofing
- Computer Vandalism
- Net Trespass
- Phishing and Credit Card Frauds

One could go on elaborating the list. The basic purpose is to highlight some of the common crimes noticed by observers of the scene.

Crimes against the Organizations include but are not limited to:

- Unauthorized access over computer systems
- Cyber-Terrorism against government organizations
- Possession of unauthorized information
- Distribution of pirated software
- Cyber-Espionage

Crimes against the Society include but are not limited to:

- Polluting the youth through indecent exposure/Child Pornography
- Trafficking
- Financial crimes
- Forgery
- On-line Gambling
- Physical Crimes relating to computer, or to hardware/software etc.
- Child Pornography

Crimes affecting data include but not limited to:

- Data diddling
- Data Leakage
- Data spying
- Scavenging

Data diddling is the most common form of crime which is carried out by input manipulation. It involves changing the data before or, during its entry into the computer. It also includes adding, changing the data with malicious intentions during or before feeding it into a computer. It does include fraudulent data input, altering the data, wrongly posting the transaction etc.

Leakage refers to illegally copying the information for ransom, blackmailing or other fraudulent purposes. Scavenging indeed refers to using information which might have been left over.

Added to this list are software crimes which arise due to affected software or a corrupted one. Similarly, there could be hardware defects as are seen in the recent case of defects in the computer chips. One finds it difficult to keep pace with such developments and more particularly be absolutely careful in applying the security patches provided for by the software companies from time to time.

We must also issue a general note of caution in respect of devices attached to innumerable utilities like cars, fridges etc. There are cases where some playthings for children place orders and the parents were hard put to get them cancelled. Ultimately, they succeeded through an intervention of the court. The ease with which routine and sometimes even complicated tasks can be resolved with the help of machines brings with it the possible dangers of subversion, and an exposure to a host of crimes.

It is now pretty obvious that many of our assumptions regarding acceptability of evidence, or rules regarding checks are undergoing some fundamental changes and with transfer of cash/making payments through mobile devices we are moving to a cashless society and countries like Kenya, China turning themselves into cashless societies and countries like India being on the way, a major transformation almost of revolutionary proportions is taking place. So are the crimes on a steep upward curve. Commercial laws or even criminal laws are slow to catch up with vastly changing practices and individuals and institutions will need to exercise utmost caution while using these services. The acts which have been modified or are in urgent need of modification are Criminal laws, Evidence Act, Bankers' Rules for Negotiable Instruments, Fraud squads, Cyber Divisions, and so on may help but our own vigil and constant watch on our transactions is of paramount importance.

Cyber-Laws: Criminal

It is against this background that we review the legal framework in some of the countries like UK and the European Union. The focus at this stage would mainly be on Criminal Law aspects and in the next section we would review the Civil Law aspects. The Computer Act of 1990, amended by the Police Act of 2006, Communication Act of 2003, Data Protection Act 2018, Investigatory Powers Act 2016, Privacy and Electronic Communications (EC) Regulations 2003, and Serious Crimes Act of 2015 cover the following areas:

- Unauthorized access to computer material
- Unauthorized access with the intent to commit or facilitate commission of further offenses
- Unauthorized acts with intent to impair or with recklessness as to impair the operations.
- It is interesting to note that in the UK an act committed outside the country by an offender, the authorities would on the return of the offender to UK treat it as if it were committed within the country. [extra territorial jurisdiction]

The police and Justice Department treat denial of access as a criminal act. Further it is stated that the act does not have to be against a specific computer or data. Further if the offense were to cause a temporary disruption and denial of service it would be considered a crime. It is noteworthy that hacking is considered as a 'terrorist act' under certain conditions:

- The use of threat is designed to influence the Government or to intimidate the public or section of the public
- The use of threat is made for advancing political, religious, racial, or ideological cause

In the UK there are a significant number of acts, directives, and regulations which come into play in such criminal acts.

- Computer Misuse Act 1990
- Police and Justice Act 2006
- Serious Crimes Act 2015
- Terrorism Act 2000
- Regulation of Investigatory Powers Act 2000
- Communications Act 2000
- Data Protection Act 2018
- Investigating Powers Act 2016
- Privacy and Electronic Communications Act [EC] Regulations Act 2003
- Human Rights Act 1998
- Crime and Courts Act 2013
- Extradition Act 2003

EU Regulatory Laws—GDPR

The EU regulations are certainly a very comprehensive attempt to achieve a degree of uniformity among the member states either directly or through an intermediary. It therefore, begins with need to have common definitions in this area. The need is to ensure a common approach to the constituent elements of criminal offenses by introducing common offenses of illegal access to an information system, illegal system interference, illegal data interference, and illegal interception. Interception includes, but is not limited to, the listening for monitoring or surveillance of the content of communications and processing of data either directly or through access and use of the information system or indirectly through electronic eaves dropping or tapping devices through technical means.

There should be penalties and criminal punishments for attacks against information systems. These penalties should be effective, proportionate to, and dissuasive and should include imprisonment or fines. Criminal penalties are also provided for cases which are not minor. A case is considered minor, if damage caused by an offense and/or the risks to public or private interests such as integrity and rights to the person is insignificant or is of such a nature that the imposition of a criminal penalty is not necessary.

A critical element in the directive is identification and reporting of threats and risks posed by cyber-attacks and other vulnerabilities of cyber-attacks. More severe penalties are proposed.

Where the attack like Ransomware is committed by a criminal organization on a large scale affecting a significant number of information systems, and where it is intended to create a bottleneck, or where cyber-attack causes serious damage or where it is directed against a critical infrastructure.

The directive proposes effective measures against identity thefts or other identity related offenses and it constitutes important element of integrated approach through horizontal union instrument.

The directive also refers to tools that can be used in order to commit the offenses laid down. Such tools include malicious software, including those creating bottlenecks. The Commission proposes to increase resilience of the information system by protecting them more effectively. Critical infrastructure should be protected and relevant measures incurring liabilities in the context of their national law where a legal person has not provided for cyber-attacks.

It rightly highlights the fact that transnational and borderless nature of information systems means that attacks against such systems have a cross-border dimension, thus underlining the urgent need for further action to approximate International Crime Law in this area. An effective fight is possible through cooperation under Mutual Legal assistance treaty between competent law enforcement bodies and judicial authorities. There is an urgent need for exchange of best practices and also to foster effective cooperation under Mutual Legal Assistance Treaty (MLAT). Specific rules against offenses are given in the directive and could be referred to by those so interested.

In 2016, the European Commission adopted a communication to strengthen Europe's Cyber Resilience System and fostering a competitive and innovative cyber-security industry. Further measures were also taken to step up cooperation in information and knowledge, preparing for Pan-European security crisis. There was a suggestion to bring forward the evolution process to increase resilience and preparedness. The idea was to examine if reforms were necessary for enhancing the capacity and capability to have a more operational and central role for strengthening the resilience of the system.

It is noteworthy that this step promotes a culture of risk management by introducing security requirements as legal obligations for key economic actors namely operators providing essential services and suppliers of key digital services. The idea is essentially to safeguard the evolving digitization of society and the proliferation of devices. There is a suggestion for ICT cyber-security certification. This is relevant as there is an increased use of technologies which require high level cyber-security namely connected and automated cars, electronic health and automation devices and control systems.

The need for cross-border cooperation is important. In June 2017 the commission provided a set of comprehensive measures that build on previous actions:

- Increasing capabilities and preparedness of member states
- Improving cooperation and coordination of member states
- Increasing EU level capabilities to complement the action of member states
- Increase awareness amongst member states
- Increasing transparency of cyber-security assurance
- Avoiding fragmentation of certification process

In looking at legislation we must see that measures proposed are such as would work in an Internet environment. The legislation devised to address a particular harm in the Internet environment either misses the mark or even worse can have unintended and undesirable side effects. Further laws preventing card offenses which have worked so far are able to contain fraud in a dynamic environment.

Cyber-Laws: Civil

The incidence of cyber-law pervades a number of areas but we would concentrate on the following aspects:

1. The Contract Aspect
2. The Intellectual Property Aspect
3. The Evidence Aspect

In a sense cyber-law encompasses the whole gamut of legal statutory provisions that affect computers and computer networks. It concerns individuals, corporate bodies and institutions which

- Are instrumental for entry into cyber-space
- Provide access to cyber-space
- Create the hardware and software which enables people to access cyber-space and
- Use their own computers to go online

Potential litigants include telephone provider companies, regulatory agencies, personal computer companies, software companies, academic bodies and firms that have a presence on the Internet. The technology scene is changing rapidly. It would not be wrong to say that anything that can be digitized is delivered to any number of users at negligible costs. The marginal cost of transport is zero. Software can and does take over tasks which normally humans would have to perform.

Questions of Jurisdiction

The first question that causes tremendous problems to the litigants is to have some understanding of the issues of a very perplexing problem of the scope of a court's power to hear particular disputes and to compel the parties involved to obey its commands. The term "jurisdiction" means many things and the broad umbrella of concepts that are covered can be summarized are as under.

- Power to legislate
- Ability to serve the defendants a notice
- Power to hear
- Power to adjudicate
- Subject matter of adjudication
- Choice of law
- Enforcement of judgments

Reference to case laws from countries like Canada, Australia, UK, or the USA becomes necessary in many cases as issues are examined from various angles and newer aspects are being considered. These cannot be ignored and over a period, fit some of our cases better than the body of decisions developed so far.

We must remember that whenever substantive legal issues are being dealt with [be it intellectual property, or privacy] jurisdiction issues would be key elements of that litigation. The Internet is a big jurisdictional problem. Events on the Internet occur everywhere but as they might not be traceable to any particular person, in particular, they become unreal. No physical Jurisdiction has a more compelling claim than any other to subject these communications and even exclusively these laws.

Contractual Aspect

The central point to remember is that the Internet is a medium or a collection of media and that can be used for contracting. With block chain technology coming in many of the problems hinging on repudiation and acceptance etc. would perhaps not come to the forefront. To us the suitable approach on the subject is Lord Denning's judgment in Entores Limited vs. Miles Far East Corporation. We quote below the relevant portions of that judgment and it should help in developing the right perspective on this issue.

> When a contract is made by post it is a clear law throughout the common law countries that the acceptance is complete as soon as the letter is into the post box and that is the place where the contract is made. There is, however, no clear rule about contracts made by telephone or by telex. Communications made by these means are instantaneous and stand on different footing. The contract is complete only when there is an acceptance of the offer. Same is the case when messages are sent through the teleprinter or telexes do not reach due to some failure of the system. The contract gets completed when the messages are repeated and when a proper acceptance received. In all the instances the man who sends the acceptance knows that it has not been received or that he has reason to know it. But suppose he thinks that it has been received. The offeror in such a case is bound because he will be stopped from saying that he did not receive the message.

We have to consider the cases where the principals are not present and that communication is through employees with limited authority. The message might have been sent after office hours or there could be some default at the recipient's end.

One could go on multiplying these difficulties. Once the message is received [section 10a of IT Act], it is to be assumed that it has been delivered. The acceptor should take the precautions to see that it has been received. In conclusion it could be said that the "offer "and acceptance of an offer may be expressed by means of electronic records. As between the "originator and an addressee" acknowledgment of receipt and concept of time and dispatch and receipt are dealt with in a genuinely different way and needs to be highlighted.

1. Unless otherwise agreed to between the originator and the addressee the dispatch of an electronic record occurs when it enters an information system outside the control of an originator.
2. Save or otherwise agreed between the originator and the addressee, the time of receipt of an electronic record shall be determined as follows.

If the addressee has designated a computer source for the purpose of receiving electronic records, (a) receipt occurs when the record enters the designated computer resource of the addressee, and (b) if the record is sent to a computer resource of the addressee that is not the designated computer resource, receipt occurs when the electronic record is retrieved by the addressee.

Evidence Aspect

The section examines the question of acceptability in civil law cases. The detailed provisions have been deliberately quoted so that staff members entrusted with the task of presenting documents have a proper understanding of the relevant provisions.

According to articles 6, 7, and 8 of UNCITRAL Model Law information wherever paper documents were required there is a substitution/ addition that digital information is acceptable. Accordingly, in India where there was a resistance initially, particularly in lower courts, digital evidence is now accepted as a matter of course. Even video conferencing in hearings are used if and when absolutely necessary. [section 65A and Section 65b of the Indian Evidence Act]

In India apart from Evidence Act, The Bankers' Book Evidence Act 1891, etc. have been suitably modified. Even digital signatures which had been considered somewhat obscure and needing elaborations are now the necessary mode for submission of certain forms, returns and documents etc.

Intellectual Property Aspect

Commerce on the Internet involves the sale of intellectual property. To promote an effective environment, sellers must know that their intellectual property will not be pirated by and that buyers must know that they are buying authentic products and not pirated copies. The issues that are likely to come up would include the following:

- Liability of online service providers
- Fair uses of Copyright material
- Effective Patent Systems
- Standards for determining valid claims
- Litigation due to trademarks
- Similarity of Internet domain names
- Liability of an intermediary, "Safe Harbor"

There is a school of thought which simply classifies cyber-crime as any form of illegal activity that takes advantage of the capabilities offered by the Internet-based systems and that exploit vulnerabilities in those systems.

Often legislation devised to address a particular harm in the Internet misses the mark or worse could have unintended or undesirable consequences or undesirable side effects.

Critical information infrastructures such as water systems, electrical grids, and payment networks as also defense Installations are often targeted by criminals and if hacked could give rise to services scarcity problems. Legislation covering such problems poses considerable challenges. Some of them are listed below.

- Modern information systems are transnational and so are crimes
- Anonymity makes attribution difficult
- The trans-national nature of the system severely hinders oversight and enforcement

The threats of cyber-crime are real and multidimensional measures are necessary to cope up with the emerging problems. We have in the Chap. 9 on Cyber-Risk Management dealt with the organization level steps that can be taken to reduce the risks of attack. However, the system is still vulnerable to such attacks at the unit level. Steps, required at this level, border on being constantly on the watch and being vigilant. Small lapses can lead to huge losses as Banks and Financial Institutions are realizing almost on a daily basis.

We begin with an examination of some of the security measures that are in vogue and are being used in practice almost universally.

Before we analyze the tools available for prevention or detection, we point out some broad trends and difficulties facing the decision makers. The field is changing too rapidly. Often senior executives are confronted with a barrage of new regulations, potential risks, and seemingly unquenchable technology budget demands. Each alone could pose a substantial risk to a firm's viability. Together they pose a potential catastrophe. It would not be wrong to say that it does at times lead to a decision paralysis. The overload experienced every day results in inaction or inappropriate actions. One must also guard against fads.

One notices certain broad trends. According to FBI, intruders were active within their victims for 160 days. Hardening IT systems to prevent between systems limiting access of authorized employees on a need to know basis and implementing centrally managed application and operating system patching policies are some of the first steps to begin decreasing this menace.

We have also to note that the attackers are going smaller and less technical. Detection is outweighing defense. IT systems are generally not able to detect an intruder until a malicious attack is committed. The attackers are in the business to make money by using the same information that is the life blood of the fintech and investment industries.

It is against this background that we should very carefully evaluate the measures suggested.

Cryptographic Tools

The details of how these tools are constructed and work are intricate, laced with mathematics and with provable and unprovable properties. The security of some tools is based on some intractable mathematical algorithms and techniques. The security of other tools cannot be proven formally but rests on the inability of experts to find and demonstrate weaknesses in the tools over the years. There are six basic tools and they are listed below.

- Symmetric [secret] key encryption
- Asymmetric key encryption
- One-way hash functions
- Message authentication codes
- Digital signatures
- Random number generators

By a careful use of these tools one seeks to design systems that can provide system security in the face of any attacks defined in associated threat model.

For asymmetric encryption, the key used to encrypt data, is a different key from that used to decrypt the data. Unlike symmetric key both for encryption and decryption, asymmetric key encryption uses two different keys. This is important because only one key needs to be kept private (secret). It is for this reason that the terms popularly used to describe this method is called "public/private" key encryption. The most widely used asymmetric key is called "RSA"—an acronym composed of the first letters of the names of its inventors. The cryptographic strength stems from the fact that it is the product of secret prime numbers. The cryptographic strength of RSA derives from the difficulty in finding the two secret prime numbers given only in their products.

Random numbers are used through algorithms, and protocols. They are used for generating keys, challenge values, pre-hashing appendages for passwords and so on. Hardware devices based on some form of physical randomness are also available. The problem with such devices is to ensure that they are working correctly.

Sole computational means for generating random numbers do not exist. However, computational means do exist for generating pseudo-random numbers. Some of the pseudo-random number generation methods employ values obtained by physical measurement of random events in a computer system such as typing rates, arbitrary mouse motions, and arrival times of I/O interrupts. Others are based on symmetric cryptography or the difficulty of hard mathematical problems such as the factoring problem. Pseudo-random number generators that produce sufficiently unpredictable values are called "Cryptographically Strong Random Number Generators".

It is not easy for banks and FIs to safeguard their networks because new vulnerabilities are discovered daily and their fixes, patches must be applied diligently to all systems. New connections to the Internet, modems, mobile devices, and virtual private networks create a multitude of new access points to a network where the risk is defined by its weakest link. Penetration testing programs are good only on the day it was tested (this is true for all security testing). No doubt, it is an excellent way of testing installed security measures, policies, and procedures and the effectiveness of a company's end-user security training programs. First the company would be able to know if intrusion detection systems are functioning effectively and what skill level is required to circumvent them. It also shows if the staff were able to detect and react to an intrusion properly. The company can find out if further training were needed. Once the penetration testing is performed, ongoing vulnerability assessment should be performed to address newly discovered exploits. The frequency of the vulnerability assessment should be performed semi-annually, and in many cases even quarterly or monthly, no matter what level of risk one was willing to accept.

So far, we have outlined the steps the organization can take as a damage control exercise. The next section points out the most frequent lapses which occur and are within the category of Controllable Items angle in the light of organizational requirements.

It is imperative that persons responsible for security and preparedness need to have a ready checklist available all the time to make sure that proper steps are organizationally taken so that the impact of cyber-attacks, data theft, and so on could be mitigated and at best eliminated.

- Proper periodic training on emerging security measures
- Ensure thorough and regular review of system access logs
- Ensure proper appreciation of the emerging disruptive trends
- Hardening of machines and systems with periodic mandatory password changes
- Deployment of new technology only after proper review of security sturdiness
- Installing applicable software patches that fix security flaws
- Regular drills to ensure restoration processes of systems from backups are sound and timely
- Ensure removal of privileged accounts no more required
- Routine internal auditing of data access

The scale and dimensions of the requirements have in recent years gone up very considerably. Therefore, it might be prudent to refer to guidance from institutions such as FBI, or periodically appointed panels by government authorities to ensure adequate protection. Equally important are the steps needed to ensure business continuity, back up data regularly, and verify the integrity of those backups

- Check your backup data regularly
- Secure your backups—use encryption and physical controls

Recent statistics show that more cyber-attacks are hitting small businesses. In fact small and medium-sized businesses (SMBs) actually suffer the lion's share of malware infections. This may look to be surprising. The numbers clearly show that these are a whole host of smaller scale attacks that are wreaking havoc on small businesses daily.

58% of malware attack victims are categorized as small businesses.

Small businesses are actually big victims when it comes to cyber-attacks. There is an increase in the number of such attacks. Frequency of such attacks is also on the increase.

Cyber-criminals are explicitly targeting small businesses. The attackers are using what could be described as "spray and pray" policy. The smaller companies get caught in the line of fire without adequate protection.

The small companies provide access to larger companies via unprotected connections. Small companies lost about U.S.$ 2mn. Damage or theft of data, disruption of normal operation. Cyber-crime will cost the world around 6 trillion of annually. Ransomware may cost $11.5 bn. 92% of malware is delivered via E-mail. Assuming that a small unit with 10 staff members gets about 8–10 messages per day. The staff will have to be on guard at least 90–100 times. Remote desktop protocol is a major mischief maker. The attacks are file less techniques and anti-viruses can't detect such attacks.

"Be careful" and do not lower your guard.

The number one priority for companies is making sure that they have malware protection and prevention in place. 81% of 5 MB report that exploits and malware have evaded their anti-virus solution.

CHAPTER 8

General Risk Management

Risk is the probability or likelihood of injury, damage, or loss in some specific environment and over some stated period of time. It involves two elements:

- Probability
- Loss Amount

Currently, the financial services industry is passing through a very critical phase. On the one hand it has to deal with the normal risks as are depicted in the diagram below. These factors have to be taken into account by FIs in normal circumstances. But they now have serious challenges to deal with because of the various factors enumerated in the earlier chapters. They have to be looked at here not in isolation but have to be viewed in totality and in many cases the decisions in respect of these have to be taken here and now. These decisions relate to closure of branches, investments in technology, reduction of staff engaged in routine functions, collaboration with a fintech partner and an uncertain and hazy technology development program. All these decisions bring with them considerable risks and would mean a huge drain on resources.

We begin with an analysis of the perception of Bankers and Insurance Management about the risks likely to emerge. While the survey of insurers pertains to the year 2017, we have to contend with 2015 survey of bankers' perceptions. These surveys (banana skin) conducted by CSIS and

V. C. Joshi, *Digital Finance, Bits and Bytes*,
https://doi.org/10.1007/978-981-15-3431-7_8

Price Waterhouse Coopers are quite representative of the Industry views and are a useful source the industry perceptions of the looming problems.

It would be noticed from the diagrammatic depiction below that these risks are interconnected and that a failure in one area could lead to an increase in non-performing assets [Indian Banks have a very serious problem on hand] could bring in other risks also. The Hexagonal representation gives a better idea about the interconnectivity of risks. For a more detailed review of risk assessment techniques and the management of risks we suggest that a reference to our Book on "Managing Indian Banks [3rd Edition]" would be found useful for those who are not familiar with these aspects. The treatment is somewhat elementary as we had noticed that even these elementary aspects were found to be somewhat difficult by a number of participants at seminars, training sessions and so on and even by some readers of the book.

We have in the first chapter of this book highlighted the various uncertainties that banks have to deal with and make their decisions on the matters referred to. Further, certain degree of caution has to be exercised regarding the assumptions on which the predictive models were based and on which banks had been depending for guidance on decision making. It is against this hazy background when a number of issues are in the melting pot that we give below the risk perceptions of bankers. We must add here a very penetrating comment by Rifkin. "The world is increasingly shaped by the digital prophets. The whole thing is premised on the idea that social media, big data, and hyperactive algorithms have fundamentally altered the ways in which we socialize, amuse ourselves learn about the world, act politically and do business. The Internet is not merely the backbone for doing business or infrastructure for economic transactions but the very oxygen that allows us to innovate, collaborate, produce and exchange goods and services."

The Internet of things is a veritable earthquake. By 2020, there would be some twenty-six billion Internet connected devices. The new architecture will help us by functioning autonomously, creating self-aware systems out of our existing real world objects that will now monitor our environment and even improve it.

Managements thus will need in-depth analysis of these various forces and come to the risk management policies. Broadly these risk prone areas could be grouped as under:

- Surge of Protectionist Policies
- Uncertain Economic Growth

- Inadequate Basic Infrastructure
- Access to Low Cost Capital
- Terrorism
- Unemployment

Other important concerns relate to Exchange Rate Volatility, Geo-Political concerns, Social Instability, Climate Change, and so on. We quote below, as a side bar (Banking Banana Skins 2015), the prioritized list as perceived by the Executives of Banks. We are aware that each institute will have its own priorities and would modify the same in the light of its own requirements. We have quoted below the relevant portion from the Report and the organization should select those which need urgent attention from its own perspective. This report describes the risk outlook for the banking industry in the final quarter of 2015—a time when the global economy and its banking system were in the advanced stages of recovery from the financial crisis, but when concerns were growing about the strength of that recovery.

Banking Banana Skins 2015 (2014 ranking in brackets)

1. Macro-economic environment (3)
2. Criminality (9)
3. Regulation (1)
4. Technology risk (4)
5. Political interference (2)
6. Quality of risk management (11)
7. Credit risk (7)
8. Conduct practices (16)
9. Pricing of risk (6)
10. Business model (–)
11. Social media (19)
12. Reputation (–)
13. Capital availability (10)
14. Interest rates (12)
15. Emerging markets (17)
16. Shadow banking (20)
17. Currency (22)
18. Liquidity (15)
19. Corporate governance (8)
20. Management incentives (21)
21. Derivatives (18)
22. Human resources (23)
23. Reliance on third parties (24)
24. Sustainability (25)

The findings are based on responses from 672 bankers, regulators, and close observers of the banking scene in 52 countries. In the opinion of these respondents, the greatest threat to the banking industry lies in the possibility that economic recovery will fail because of the huge—and in many cases rising—weight of debt in all the main sectors: sovereign, corporate, and consumer. There are also strong concerns about economic weakness in developing economies, and uncertainty surrounding central banks' monetary policies.

A senior banking supervisor said "Higher indebtedness brings greater financial fragility. Regulators and banks have made some progress in reducing leverage in the banking sector. But it remains high nonetheless. And the increasing indebtedness of borrowers leaves banks vulnerable in the face of economic shocks."

Given such views, one of the strongest risks is concern about the quality of banks' risk management, which rose from No. 11 in 2014 to No. 6 in this survey. Although much work has been done by banks and their regulators to strengthen risk controls, there is a sense that banks have still not adequately addressed not just the scale of risk but also, it's changing nature. The changing nature of risk is summed up by the sharp rise in concern about Criminality (up from No. 9 to No. 2), chiefly because of the alarming spread of cyber-crime in an increasingly borderless market, particularly data theft. This is closely associated with Technology risk (No. 4) where underinvestment and obsolescence, and banks' growing exposure to competition from fintech companies, now presents major challenge.

Another strong rise in the area of risk management is Conduct Practices (up from No. 16 to No. 8) because of what is perceived to be the banks' failure to achieve "culture change" in the management of their business practices despite strong regulatory pressure and heavy fines. One banker described unethical business practices as a "perennial risk", which won't go away as we make money out of people who don't pay money or pay the loans in a timely manner.

Even so, Reputational risk did not rank as high as might be expected (No. 12) because of the view that this is one risk to which there is little downside. Political interference in banking is seen to be declining (down from No. 2 last year to No. 5) and excessive regulation, long a high-ranking risk, slipped from the top position last year to No. 3. The most threatening riser in this area is Social Media (up from No. 19 to No. 11) with its power to damage bank reputations with or without sound evidence.

A number of risks which were associated with the financial crisis have continued to recede. Among them are the Pricing of risk (i.e. aggressive underpricing to achieve competitive advantage) which went down from No. 6 to No. 9, the availability of capital to strengthen bank Balance Sheets (down from No. 10 to No. 13), and Liquidity risk (down from No.15 to No. 18) because of the commitment by central banks to keep funding markets afloat. Interest rate risk was also low at No. 14 despite the long-anticipated end to quantitative easing, banks have had plenty of time to prepare for it, though it will be a first-time experience for the industry and its impact cannot be predicted with any certainty.

Two notable risers are Emerging Markets (up from No. 17 to No. 15) where concern focuses on the prospects for China and the impact of weak commodity prices on a string of dependent economies, and Shadow Banking (up from No. 20 to No. 16), the unregulated (and therefore potentially dangerous) para-financial sector whose growth is seen to be fueled by excessive regulation of mainstream suppliers. Institutional risks to banks show a mixed trend. The good news is that the risk of poor corporate governance has fallen sharply from No. 8 to No. 19 following recent improvements, though there is a thread of concern that boards may no longer be physically capable of staying on top of issues in their increasingly complex and fast-moving institutions. The bad news is that concern is rising over the viability of bank Business model (No. 10) when changing structures, technologies, and markets demand constant adaptation.

Worthy of comment among the very low ranked risks is sustainability, or environment-associated risk at No. 24. Although a number of respondents saw a connection between banks and their potentially exposed clients here, the broad perception is that banks have little to fear from environmental threats, and would, in any case, be able to adapt.

Risk Management for E-Banking and E-Insurance

We now specifically look at Banking and Insurance Industries' attempts at controlling and managing these risks [E-banking and E-insurance]. We would particularly highlight two features. These industry groups are most reluctant to disclose any intrusions into their systems. The reluctance to do so stems from fears about further attacks and about adverse publicity. The very fact that the system could be tampered with, is enough to lead to a panic reaction amongst the clients.

The South-East Asian Crisis and the Baring Bank debacle were perhaps the immediate causes for banks and the supervisors to come together to evolve sound policies for this vital area of management for the financial service industry. It is indeed heartening that the problem is being looked at on a global level and that most of the countries are not only examining these problems but are also concerned with developing appropriate strategies suited to their conditions. A particularly encouraging feature is that whenever there are differences of views amongst Central Regulators these are aired and even made available on their web sites for comments. Further the organizations, which have framed these rules, do not claim that these are "model" rules and that they need to be copied in to.

The following figure describes the various forces that have to be taken into consideration (Fig. 8.1).

We now begin with a summary of recommendations made by Bank for International Settlement. These are part of the total set of recommendations for "Risk Management" and need to be viewed in that context.

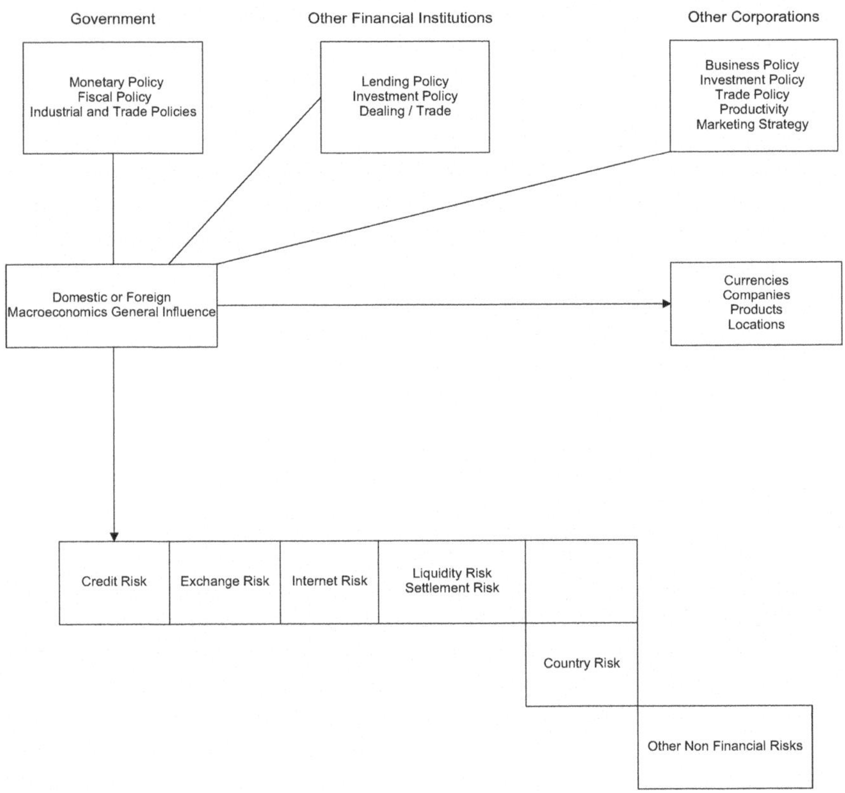

Fig. 8.1 Analysis of risk. (Source: Author)

A bank or financial institute developing the E-trade channel must be equally careful about the total apparatus it has for the risk management function. E banking must be a part of that scheme. Further organizations like the Federal Deposit Insurance Corporation of USA also come out with specific guide lines and organizations could certainly take advantage of these recommendations.

The recommendations are summarized below and we strongly advocate a reference to the original document for a proper appreciation of the suggestions made. Obviously, these could be looked on as tried and tested measures. BIS is quite right in asserting that fulfilling detailed risk management requirements must not be counter-productive. Each bank's risk profile is different and requires a tailored approach for risk mitigation appropriate for the scale of E-banking operations, the materiality of risks present and the institute's willingness and ability to manage the risks. This does imply that one-size fits all approach to E-banking risk management may not be quite suited. The risk management efforts broadly fall into three groups:

- Management Oversight
  Effective management oversight of the risks associated with E-banking needs to be in place and risk management should be integrated with overall risk management. There must be explicit, informed, and documented strategic decisions covering specific accountabilities, policies, and controls, to address risks. Key aspects of security control process must be covered.
- Security Controls
  These should include appropriate control processes such as
  - Authentication of E-banking customers
  - Non-repudiation and accountability for E-banking transactions
  - Appropriate measures for segregation of duties
  - Data integrity of E-banking transactions, records, and information
  - Establishment of clear audit trails for E-banking transactions
  - Confidentiality of key banking transactions
  - Legal and Reputational Risk Management Principles
  - Appropriate disclosures for E-banking services
  - Privacy of customer information

- Capacity, business continuity and
- Contingency planning to ensure availability of E-banking services
- Indent response planning

- Due Diligence
  Comprehensive due diligence and management oversight processes for outsourcing relations and third-party dependencies.

Against the backdrop of information given above the committee has developed 14 key risk management principles and for the sake of easy reference they are given below:

1. Management Oversight
2. Management of outsourcing and third-party dependencies
3. Segregation of duties
4. Proper authorization measures and controls
5. Clear audit trails
6. Authentication of all entities, counterparts, and data
7. Non-repudiation of E-banking transactions
8. Comprehensive security
9. Integrity of banking transactions, records, and information
10. Appropriate disclosure for E-banking services
11. Confidentiality and privacy of customer information
12. Business continuity and contingency planning
13. Incident response planning
14. Role of supervisors

The Insurance Sector

We would now look at some of the principles enunciated by the International Association of Insurance Supervisors. They have offered some background material and the same needs to be taken note of. Companies should be conscious of strategic risks associated with an Internet strategy. These risks are critical and would be more so when new products designed for sale on the Internet reach the market. One has also to bear in mind the new underwriting opportunities that would come up.

They have highlighted one aspect and that needs to be brought out. The risks posed by electronic commerce that are new or different in scale or impact from traditional business conducted through other distribution channels must be critically examined. Reputations are at stake as mistakes can multiply and spread quickly.

Strategic Risks

These risks arise when a company engaging in new business strategy, does not think through the implications that the decision on electronic commerce will have on other parts of the organization or the company as a whole. Without such a plan the risks of mistakes occurring increases and the chances of the strategy succeeding decrease.

The impact on the solvency should be the overreaching consideration in the analysis. In addition, the company should be wary that

- The global nature and rapid development and growth of electronic commerce will put pressure on its planning and implementation of online operations, in particular, product design and technological applications.
- Internet is an efficient way of doing business but it is far from cost free. System costs and maintaining customer awareness of the web site may involve significant advertising costs.
- Brand loyalty may evaporate in the face of competition. Customers could switch their business from one to the other company.
- There is a danger of some customers being neglected. There is an equal danger that research, product innovation, data security and even risk management may be neglected;
- The speed of processing may complicate management of information;
- Dangers of adverse selection could increase and there could be inadequate disclosure by the customers.
- It is the responsibility of the Board to choose strategies that reflect the company's desired risk profile, functional capabilities and solvency. It must decide how its Internet strategy will influence the company's philosophy, the way it conducts business and its financial situation.

Without a well thought out strategy, the decision to engage in electronic commerce may result in an unwarranted increase in risks at the operational level and an unproductive drain on resources.

Operational Risks

These relate to risks that arise as a result a failure or default in the information technology infrastructure. There could even be deficiencies in the structure available. It may not:

- have the capacity to handle increased traffic and process transaction and volume;
- be scalable;
- be accessible all the time due to a lack of fault tolerant technology;
- be secure from internal and external disruption;
- be accessible, compatible, or interoperable in every market;
- have appropriate policies and controls in place for third-party vendors. Adequate scrutiny of the service provider's operational viability, financial liquidity, and project management skills.

Transaction Risks

Transaction risks arise on account of an unauthorized alteration or modification to texts, information or data transmitted over the computer network between an insurer and the client or vice versa. In electronic commerce these risks arise mainly on account of technology. This risk also includes information, which is hosted on the server or web site of a "partner" third party.

Data Security Risks

These risks arise due to losses, unintentional changes, or leaks of information or data in computer systems. These could be broadly divided into two categories. It could be within the company system itself. Incompatibility of the data systems or incompatibility of the part of the data system information leaks or information loss may be the cause for such risks.

The external links could lead to data breaks. A customer's personal data may be illegally accessed. These could complicate and, in some cases, negate the company's ability to authenticate information and data. Information concerning an insurance contract may be changed without authorization after the system has been broken into. A company's reputation may suffer.

Connectivity Risks

Failure in one part of the system may impact all or other parts of the system. If any part of the Internet's operational system is damaged as a result of intentional or negligent actions the company may fail to provide service to clients.

Conduct of Business Risks

The laws and regulations are developed with the view that business will be conducted on a person to person basis, with proper documentation. Electronic commerce poses new issues with attendant risks, such as:

- Authenticating the identity of a customer
- Verifying and maintaining the security of electronic documents and signatures
- Notification of contract-related information must safeguard the interests of the client and the company
- Format and presentations must be such that disclosure and disclaimer requirements are met
- Policyholders to be provided with a proof acceptable to regulators or other third parties
- Acceptance of electronic payments in lieu of checks, drafts, or cash;
- Meeting record retention requirements

The supervisors apprehend that a host of legal issues including the status of the insurer, location of the company and, therefore, by whom and how it would be supervised, the applicable laws etc. would sooner or later come up. They are also afraid that the clients may not know all the risks involved and when and if a problem arises it may be too late even for a proper remedy to be found.

Alternate Systems of Trading

Securities and Exchange Board of India are far more specific and have even indicated the use of specific technology for risk management. We give below a summary of their major conclusions:

- Exchanges must ensure that brokers have a system-based control on the trading limits of clients, and their exposures. There must be pre-defined limits on the exposure and turnover of each client.
- The systems should be such that client risks could be immediately assessed and that the client would be informed within a reasonable time frame.
- The reports on margin requirements, payment, and delivery, should be made known to the client through the system
- Contract notes must be issued within 24 hrs. or as per existing rules
- No cross trades to be undertaken
- The other rules applicable to brokers would, no doubt, continue to operate.
- Documents should be authenticated through digital signature, electronic certification, etc.

The security measures as shown below are mandatory for all Internet-based trading systems:

- User ID, first level passwords, automatic expiry of passwords, and reinitializing access on entering fresh passwords.
- All transaction logs with proper audit trails and facilities to be maintained.
- Suitable firewalls between trading setup connected to the exchange system and the Internet trading system
- Secured Socket Level Security for server access through Internet

SEBI has gone a step further and recommended the following: (a) Microprocessor-based smart cards; (b) Dynamic password; (c) 64-bit/128-bit encryption and finally (d) Second Level password.

Standards for interface between the brokers and clients have also been prescribed.

The rules also give detailed instructions to brokers to use the same logic/priorities used by exchanges to treat client orders. Brokers are also to maintain all activities/alerts log with audit trail facility. There has to be a unique numbering system, which is internally generated.

We have treated the risk management suggestions for various sectors as if they are part apart. It would be easily seen that there is a considerable overlap and that many suggestions by Insurance Regulators would be equally applicable to banking/broking.

To summarize, we would add that Chap. 9 on Cyber-Risk Management details specific risks arising from criminal activities. We have included therein detailed suggestions on steps to be taken. Many of the requirements can be taken care of by technology. We have refrained from going into these in great details as Management would have to take these decisions themselves depending on their specific requirements. Further, one is also aware that the developments are so fast that the suggestions could be outmoded before they are made. We have covered some of the aspects in in the chapter on cyber-security and some details on computer crimes bring home the message for greater attention to risk management.

CHAPTER 9

Cyber-Risk Management

We have in the previous chapter discussed problems relating to risk management in general. We are, however, adding this special chapter on Cyber-Risk Management because of the huge losses suffered by Financial Institutions and other organizations on account of cyber-attacks. The maximum attacks have been suffered by the FIS. One way of dealing with this uncontrollable risk is to see that vulnerabilities in other areas are controlled to the maximum extent possible and then pay attention in a concentrated manner on this area.

In today's context organizations are concerned not with "if and when" the attack would take place but with the problem of how big the attack would be. Given that any organization small or big is likely to be subjected to such attacks, organizations have to take steps to ensure that they try and build up the resilience necessary for a quick recovery and restoration of operations. We have seen in the chapter on cyber-crimes what disruptions are likely to result. Therefore, time and resources spent on preparedness for recovery should be considered as an important and necessary step.

ISO/IEC defines "cyber-security" or "cyber-space security" as the preservation of confidentiality, integrity, and availability of information in the cyber-space. Cyber-space is defined as the complex environment resulting from the interaction of people, software services on the Internet by means of technology devices and networks connected to it and which does not exist in any physical form.

V. C. Joshi, *Digital Finance, Bits and Bytes*,
https://doi.org/10.1007/978-981-15-3431-7_9

The problem with definitions is that any wide definition results in wider coverage but could lead to confusion in responsibilities. A narrow definition, on the other hand, results in the creation of another risk management activity and may not receive the focused and continuous attention it deserves. We however feel that it is necessary to have a wider definition and the organizations should spread the security net wide. It is not a matter for mere regulatory compliance. It is far more important to see that responsibilities are clearly defined and that it is never far from the top management radar screens.

Very broadly put, these crimes can be seen to be encompassed in the following three categories.

- Data Breaches
- Ransom Demands
- Distributed Denial of service

In an increasingly digitized world data resides in cloud, on mobile phones and in devices connected to Internet of things that is devices which automatically interact with other machines, say, computers programmed to order your milk when supplies in the fridge reach a given level.

Cyber-risks emanate from various sources both national and those operating from overseas centers. The perpetrators, shown below, could be located anywhere. The following are some of the frequently identified sources.

- Criminal Organizations
- Disgruntled employees seeking revenge
- Frauds perpetrated by employees seeking either gains or even showing off their "hacking" skills
- Accidental breaches
- Suppliers or contractors to whom work might have been outsourced and where their systems are not robust enough
- Corporate Espionage
- Ideology groups

We would particularly add that the organized crime groups (referred to above) operate with multiple divisions and could be considered as specialists in areas such as management hacking, coding, server administration, and money laundering**Error! Bookmark not defined.**. Such groups can conduct attacks on a great scale and with a high degree of sophistication and carry these out against specific firms and with utmost precautions so that it becomes difficult to catch the perpetrators.

It should be remembered that data theft, hacking, and disruption of IT services are outlawed activities and that any such crime is difficult to detect. Further execution of such crimes is not an expensive proposition. We list below known facets about some of the other likely perpetrators listed above.

- Risk from Employees

These risks can be considered from two different perspectives.

1. Threats
2. Human Errors

The threat part can be dealt with by fencing off sensitive data, intellectual property, and strategies both general and specific relating to detection and future planning. Such problems can arise anywhere and we are aware that such crimes arising at senior management levels are hard to trace and tackle. Executives at senior management level have access to important and sensitive data/information and they could cause serious problems if they feel that they have been wronged/slighted for some reason(s).

- Outsourcing of Activities

Obviously, this turns out to be a vulnerable area. Jobs outsourced would create a number of crime prone avenues. The firms/corporations to whom such work is assigned may not live up to the required standards if it were a small or medium organization. They may not be in a position to afford the expenses for risk management. For them the cost and benefit analysis may show that the costs may outweigh the benefits or that they are too small to bear the required expenses of cyber-risks management. We quote below a unique case of hacking a petroleum company. The hackers could not succeed in the process. They however found out that the company employees ordered food from a Chinese takeaway nearby. The Chinese restaurant was hacked and through it the petroleum company.

In the next section we turn our attention to management of cyber-risks.

At the outset we must issue a general warning. During the discussion at seminars we are told that the organization has insured against the risks and that losses could be mitigated. But let us not forget that there are non-insurable losses like reputational loss which could, in today's environment (when trust in the Financial Institutions is at a low ebb) turn out to be a major loss. Further if the insurance cover leads to a sense of complacency it would be a serious matter for the C-suite to worry about. Let it also not be forgotten that insurance companies lay down certain compliance requirements/conditions or even levy higher premium for the same set of risks. The National Association of Commissioners for Insurance have issued guidelines for insurers and the companies will have to follow these when issuing the policies.

Risk Management Programs for Information Risk Management

It is becoming extremely important for agents/insurers to pay great attention to security. They have to make sure that they are putting together the best program for information risk management. It does involve additional reporting, additional assessment, and even to take a look at their vendors They may even suggest appropriate program for information risks management in the organizations so that it helps the insurers and the customers also.

The law expects agents/insurers to develop a close relationship with their customers through consumer training and to ensure the use of best practices.

Organizational Response

The regulatory authorities have in many cases stipulated certain compliance standards, developed regulatory rules for observance and have gone to the extent of levying penalties for such noncompliance. European Union, the Financial services Authority in England have, for institutions under their jurisdiction, issued very specific guidelines to be followed by the institutions and we would discuss those in the chapter on Regulation. We give below the general guidelines for the use of Financial Institutions which are essential for maintaining and promoting financial stability and economic growth. If not properly managed, FIs can be sources of financial shock, such as liquidity dislocations and credit losses, or a major channel through which these shocks are transmitted across domestic and international financial markets. In this context, the level of cyber-resilience, which contributes to an FI's operational resilience, can be a decisive factor in the overall resilience of the financial system and the broader economy.

The safe and efficient operation of financial market infrastructures enhances their cyber-resilience.

Specifically, the risk management categories are governance, identification, protection, detection, and response and recovery. The overarching components are testing, situational awareness, and learning and evolving. In order to achieve resilience objectives, investments across these guidance categories can be mutually reinforcing and should be considered together.

While the guidance is directly aimed at FIs, it is important for them to ensure that they cooperate not merely with the concerned authorities but also with others in the industry. In order to achieve resilience objective, investments across these guidance categories should be mutually reinforcing and ought to be considered together.

We reiterate that it is important for FIs to take on an active role in outreach to their participants and other relevant stakeholders to promote understanding and support of resilience objectives and their implementation. Given the extensive interconnections in the financial system, the cyber-resilience of an FI is in part dependent on that of interconnected FIs, of service providers and of the participants.

Collaboration

Effective solutions may necessitate collaboration between FIs and their stakeholders as they seek to strengthen their own cyber-resilience. Efforts to coordinate the design of resilience solutions may bring enhanced strategies forward in a more timely and efficient way. The outcome of such collaboration should be considered in their individual and collective strategic planning. Because the cyber-resilience of FIs supports broader financial stability objectives and in the light of significant interdependencies in clearing and settlement processes, it is important for authorities to cooperate, recognizing that such cooperation may help authorities consider, where appropriate, consistency of direction in their oversight and supervision of both FIs and their relevant stakeholders. Moreover, authorities and FIs may need to call upon technology companies and other firms to help identify and develop efficient and effective solutions.

Cyber-Security Assessment Tool

To complete the assessment management should first assesses the institution's inherent risk profile based on five categories:

- Technologies and connection types
- Delivery channels
- Online mobile products/services
- Organizational characteristics
- External threats

The management of the institution's cyber-security maturity levels broadly comprises the following:

- Cyber-risk management and oversight
- Threat intelligence and collaboration
- Cyber-security controls
- External dependency management
- Cyber-incident manager and -resilience

Inherent risk levels and maturity levels should be reviewed and the institute can then identify its maturity levels and their suitability appropriate in relation to its risk. The institute could then reduce the risk or increase maturity levels. Cyber-security is a process of protecting information by preventing, detecting, and responding to attacks. Protecting infrastructure and information assets are the two major aspects.

Cyber-incidents lead to financial, operational, legal, and reputational risks being suffered. Cyber-incidents, no doubt, can significantly impact capital and earnings.

Costs may include forensic investigations, P R Campaigns, legal fees, consumer credit monitoring, and technology changes. Cyber-security must be integrated throughout the institution's part of enterprise-wide governance process, and should cover information security program, business continuity, and third-party risk management.

1. The assessment is designed to provide a measurable and repeatable process adequate for the institute's level of cyber-security risk and preparedness.

2. Cyber-security maturity—current state of cyber-security preparedness as represented by maturity levels. The institute should have such an exercise periodically on an enterprise level particularly while introducing new products.
3. The Management should review risk profile, whenever new products, services, or initiatives enterprise wide are introduced. Management ought to review risk profile and to understand which policies, procedures, processes, and controls are in place and where gaps may exist. Determine the maturity levels and then draw up the required action plan.
4. New products, services, or initiatives

Inherent Risk Profile—Comprises certain types of connections and technologies that pose a challenge and higher inherent risks depending on complexity and maturity, connections and nature of specific products and services.

The risk profile may vary as under:

- Least inherent risk
- Minimal inherent risk
- Moderate inherent risk
- Significant
- Most inherent risk

Delivery channels—Greater the variety and number of channels, inherent risk increases with on-line/mobile products. With various payment services included, the risks increase considerably. Table 9.1 shows different technologies and connections types as well as the levels of associated risk.

The next step consists of determining maturity levels

Domain 1: Cyber-Risk Management and oversight
Domain 2: Threat intelligence and collaboration
Domain 3: Cyber-Security Control
Domain 4: External Dependency Management
Domain 5: Cyber-Incident Management and resilience

Table 9.1 External threats

Category: Technologies and connection types	*Risk level*				
	Least	*Minimum*	*Moderate*	*Significant*	*Most*
Total number of Internet service provider (ISP) connections (including branch connections)	No connections	Minimal complexity (1–20 connections)	Moderate complexity (21–100 connections)	Significant complexity (101–200 connections)	Substantial complexity (>200 connections)
Unsecured external connections, number of connections not users (e.g., file transfer protocol (FTP), Telnet, rlogin)	None	Few instances of unsecured connections (1–5)	Several instances of unsecured connections (6–10)	Significant instances of unsecured connections (11–25)	Substantial instances of unsecured connections (>25)
Wireless network access	No wireless access	Separate access points for guest wireless and corporate wireless	Guest and corporate wireless network access are logically separated; limited number of users and access points (1–250 users; 1–25 access points)	Wireless corporate network access; significant number of users and access points (251–1,000 users; 26–100 access points)	Wireless corporate network access; all employees have access; substantial number of access points (>1,000 users; >100 access points)

Source: FFIEC Cyber-Security Assessment Tool: Federal Financial Examination Council. https://www.ffiec.gov/pdf/cybersecurity/FFIEC_CAT_May_2017.pdf

Sound Governance

Consistent with effective management of other forms of risk faced by an organization, sound governance is the key. Cyber-governance refers to the arrangements the FI has put in place to establish, implement, and review its approach to managing cyber-risks. Effective governance should start with a clear and comprehensive cyber-resilience framework that accords a high priority to the safety and efficiency of the FI's operations while supporting broader financial stability objectives. The framework should be guided by a cyber-resilience strategy, and define how the FI's cyber-resilience objectives are determined. They should take an active role in outreach to their participants and other relevant stakeholders to promote understanding and support of resilience objectives and their implementation. Given the extensive interconnections in the financial system, the cyber-resilience of a FI is in part dependent on that of interconnected FIs, of service providers and of the participants.

Steps FIs need to take in this behalf:

- Objectives must be clearly determined and the reasons should be outlined to various end users
- Estimates of people, processes, and necessary technology must be quickly in place
- A clear identification of key business functions, information assets, and more particularly sensitive "data sets"
- Protection of confidentiality, integrity, and availability and the means for achieving these through appropriate controls, systems, and information practices to prevent, to limit, and to contain the impact of cyber-incidents
- Detections and recurrence of anomalies and events

Far more important is the resumption within a matter of hours. Obligations are to be settled within a given value date. Systems testing prior to this are a must. The impact and situational awareness can never be overemphasized.

We are often asked by some skeptical executives about the efficacy of such programs. They rightly feel that the measures that are proposed do not take into account the fact that it is like aiming at a bird which is not only indistinct but also moving in a wayward fashion. The organizations are totally in the dark about by whom, when, and where an attack is likely.

The only way the organization can respond is to be in a state of readiness all the time. Unfortunately warding off such attacks is not the only function so goes the argument. But we cannot forget that bad reputation is equally harmful and reputational risk is perennially present. Attention to myriad functions is no doubt a critical activity but the risk management areas are a shade more important. Any slackening of attention could be very harmful.

We do not mean to suggest that the organizations could neglect or pay less attention to such threats because they are indistinct. A 24 × 7 vigil is the mantra for prevention of reputational risk.

Organizations have to be in a state of readiness and are expected to carry out stress tests and also work actively and try to find out who the enemy is how best one can anticipate his activities so that the enemy is outwitted. The FIs could undertake a stress test and assess their weaknesses and take advance precautions to plug the loopholes.

Data Breaches

It refers to an incident that results in confirmed disclosure—not just potential disclosure of data to an unauthorized party. Even a single incident is a breach of integrity, confidentiality, or availability of information of an asset. Verizon Report on Data breaches [2018, Page 5] broadly details the actors and the classification of perpetrators is as under:

75% of the incidents that occurred were perpetuated by outsiders while 25% were the handiwork of insiders. 62% of such incidents could be defined as hacking attacks while almost 51% could be attributed to malware. It is indeed surprising that 81% of hacking related breaches occurred because of weak passwords being leveraged. One could very broadly say that about 66% of these events occurred because of malware that was installed via malicious E-mail attachments. There were almost 1,000 incidents in the financial sector and of these 475 were breaches.

It would be useful to note that denial of service, web applications attacks, and card skimming represent 58% of all security incidents. 94% of these attacks were by external agencies. The cyber-security landscape is becoming perilous by the day. The important step to be taken is to have national level insight and oversight. The need for chief Digital Security Officer is of paramount importance and amongst his other functions developing a national level defense strategy is immediate and of paramount importance.

It must be stated that there are other complimentary tools like

- IT governance policies
- Information Security
- IT Audit
- Business continuity Planning
- Customer Awareness programs

SEC CEO Marshall S. Sprung said, "Firms must adopt written policies to protect their client's private information and they need to anticipate potential cyber-security events and have clear procedures in place rather than waiting to react once a breach occurs."

A cyber-security breach is immediately transmitted through social media and the Internet and creates/threatens reputational risk. Loss of reputation could lead to a loss of customers and stake holders trust and finally to a loss of revenue and a higher level of regulatory scrutiny while posting threat to SENIOR management.

The "WannaCry" attack was preventable. The attack took advantage of vulnerability in windows software for which Microsoft had released a software patch two months prior to the attack. But most of the businesses had not updated their versions of windows. The attack shows how easy it is to launch a malware on global scale by using a simple easily available ransomware as a service. Being resilient as we have already suggested means taking a hit and to recover quickly.

- Install the latest security updates for operating system.
- Ensure that the system does not have any unnecessary connections on the computer.
- No user should ever get administrative access. Access needs to be segmented.
- Implementing a functional data backup and recovery plan. Copies of proprietary data need to be stored in secure and separate locations.
- All E-mail messages need to be scrutinized to see that there are no unsolicited messages.
- Develop, institute, and practice employee education program to identify scams, malicious links etc.
- Have penetration test at least once every year.
- Finally, like hackers we must innovate.

It needs to be mentioned that periodic audit and strategic assessment of threats and vulnerabilities to identify the gaps must be undertaken. The United States National Institute of standards and technology's "Cyber-Security Framework" suggests the following elements.

- Identify
- Protect
- Detect
- Respond
- Recover

The tasks are stupendous. Private Sector and Governments must come together to encourage innovation in security technology and the best defense system. One cannot avoid mentioning that laws protecting private and public networks could deter many cyber-hackers.

We conclude with an example of such a joint partnership endeavor in preventing payment frauds.

In payments industry, by harnessing the power of data an attempt was made to protect consumers. Every transaction that flows through visa Network is analyzed against 500 data elements to determine risk for fraud and help the card issuer decide whether to approve or decline a purchase. But as commerce becomes increasingly digital across mobile, tablet, wearable electronics, and other connected devices, we need to upgrade data pipes to be able to analyze information more complex than simple passwords.

Contextual data such as device identification, biometrics geolocation, browsing behavior has been made possible by the growth of connected devices. This data is powerfully predictive of fraudulent or legitimate transaction.

Building a foundation of privacy and security requires that organizations recognize this problem and correct their approach. It necessitates that we innovate and invest in ways to harness the power of connected devices and intelligent data to help prevent frauds. Conditions are changing rapidly and we must remember that poachers are not limiting their options.

2018 Cyber-Risk Landscape

Cyber-risk management and awareness continue to improve. But many organizations still lag on implementing fundamental risk management and mitigation measures. Hackers on the other hand, are perpetually refining their methods and tools in the cyber-crime area such as

- To stay ahead
- To steal data
- To sow discord
- To stay profitable

With many of the companies becoming more alert, cyber-security concerns are also getting more nuanced. Managing such complex dynamics requires a deeper understanding of tactics, tools, and trends. It would be useful for the managements to be aware of the broader trends in this behalf.

Ransomware is a dominant crime tool. Lower execution costs, high returns, and minimal repercussions for the criminals make it highly attractive for them. The threat continues to broaden with ransomware as a service for sale on Dark Web. Strange as it may seem, the sale of ransomware software increased by 2500% to $5.2 million. Accenture's I Defense notes 65 new areas and more particularly health care institutes as their major targets—"WannaCry" and "Not Petym". The fact that both these systems reach critical infrastructure, leads us to believe that more and more spillover will occur along with the disruption and financial loss. The criminals would continue to threaten industrial networks for extortion gains.

Regulation

Regulatory bodies continue to move toward adopting and enforcing criminal liability for cyber-security failures. Compliance now becomes complex and costly proposition. Data protection laws now require tighter security practices. The requirements are rigorous and major fines are levied for violations. More and more investments are called for proactive cyber-risk management effort. Simulating real world attack scenarios, refining existing defenses and security and response procedures are getting more and more complex. In fact, the National Institute for Standards in USA is requesting the US government to harmonize regulatory practices. This particular trend is global and compliance is becoming a more complex and costly proposition. Security practices sometimes do vary according to the jurisdiction in which they are operating and/or storing data or processing data for their customers. According to Accenture's Defense Threat report, the threat actors who gain unauthorized access to confidential information may choose to extort organizations beholden to General Data Protection Regulation (GDPR) rather than leak data. Enforcement fines can be as high as €20 million or 4% of annual global turnover whichever is higher.

Businesses must try to preempt these issues, respecting users' privacy, responsibly using consumer data and content to enhance services. They must set limits on how long they can and should hold the data. It is equally important for them to give a prompt notification for the breached entities. NY State Department for Financial Services sets a 72 hours limit.

Business E-mail Compromise

Business E-mail compromise schemes consistently succeed because of simple social engineering and phishing skills required of fraudsters. This means quick money for fraudsters and losses for the business. It is projected that this kind of dirty business will jump up from US $5.4 billion to more than $9 billion. Equally noteworthy is the danger from impersonation of company executives. E-mail security risk assessment report shows that organizations should look to malware attachments and dangerous files as the main sources for such crimes. And yet business impersonation attacks and E-mail compromises scheme increased by about 50% during the last two or three years. Impersonation attacks are an easy way and curiously security measures could not detect them. Two out of three IT Executives had to deal with security incidents. The attackers know that impersonation attacks are an easy way to dupe unsuspecting victims by gaining trust through a combination of social engineering and technical means.

IoT Devices

These continue to be rapidly developed but with insufficient security. IoT ties into the vulnerabilities in the supply chain both physically and technically. It can easily get into their customer's network. Hackers getting access to supplier's network through unsecured devices and adding the customer's network to it is the normal modus operandi. Perhaps the way out could be for large organizations to broaden third party risk management programs and frequent due diligence processes so that they can easily account for weaknesses in vendor IoT security. Small and Medium Businesses (SMBs) will have to improve and document their cyber-security measures.

Third Party Supply Chains

Vulnerabilities introduced by vendors and third parties in the supply chains are an equally important source for such crimes. Leveraging service providers' access to the customer's systems and data continue to demand constant scrutiny and access management. Hackers can create a back-door entry into many enterprises by injecting tweaked file into updates of any software and using that entry point to spread the malware through the victim's entire network. Attackers can target even one organization, and in the process gaining a foothold to compromise hundreds and thousands more.

Geo Political Conflict

Tensions on borders like the Korean Peninsula, Russians targeting Ukraine and western democracies, and conflict between Iran and Saudi Arabia have been responsible for innumerable threat activities.

At a hearing of US Senate Armed forces Committee, the Director of Defense Intelligence Agency described exploitation of insecure IoT devices as one of the two most emerging cyber-threats to national Security. Therefore, there is a need for secure and resilient products and services. The IoT Cyber-Security Act 2019 requires National Institute of Standards and Technology to issue recommendations for secure development, identity management and configuration management for IoT devices. The contractors must adopt a coordinated vulnerability disclosure policy.

We now turn our attention to EU regulations and more particularly article 5 of the General Data Protection Regulation (GDPR). Very often, during discussion on the subject there is a vehement criticism of the hefty fines levied under these provisions. We must say that in the whole discussion, the customer whose data is compromised, was totally ignored. We can't forget that it is the organization which wants to take advantage of the fact that they have access to such data because the customer(s) has reposed the trust into the organization. A breach in the organization's systems leads to considerable harassment to hundreds of customers. The organizations will take utmost care if and only if they realize that protection to the customers is the sacred task entrusted to them.

Article 5 of the EU directive sets out seven key principles which lie at the heart of the general data protection regime. It requires that personal data shall be

- Processed lawfully, fairly, and in a transparent manner in relation to every individual (lawfulness, fairness, and transparency)
- Collected for specified, explicit, and legitimate purposes and not processed further in a manner that is incompatible with those purposes. Uses for public interest, scientific or historical research or statistical purposes shall not be considered to be incompatible.
- Adequate, relevant, and limited to what is necessary in relation to the purpose for which they are processed.
- Accurate and where necessary kept up-to-date. Weeding out inaccurate data is a must.
- Kept in a form which permits identification of subjects for no longer than is necessary for which personal data is processed.
- Processed in a manner that ensures appropriate security of the personal data against inappropriate (unlawful processing), accidental loss, destruction, or damage.

Controller shall be responsible for and be responsible to demonstrate compliance with the above mentioned.

Various reports and surveys of board members and non-IT senior management show that almost all the board members fail to understand these risks. They lack familiarity with specific technical aspects or did not have even general expertise in cyber-security. The reliance on consultants or insurance companies for making good the cyber-crime losses are their main defense.

Many firms fail to indicate the dos and don'ts and even to join the dots between cyber and other conduct issues that may occur through cyber-channels. It is surprising that many firms are not aware that many of their risks can be mitigated (even the ones from insiders) in various ways. These are:

- Improve the logical access control
- Classify data according to its sensitivity (commercial value or other specific characteristics and company specific special initiatives)

As a policy, the board which has ultimate responsibility should ensure that cyber-controls are designed to meet standards of resilience. They must constantly review the institution's controls to meet these threats. Lastly were an attack to be successful, the board has to ensure that the institution's plans are clear, well designed and that the recovery takes place quickly.

The various survey reports clearly bring out that organizations have much to do in implementing not merely the technical but even organizational measures required to defend against cyber-risks.

It is against this background that the Basel Committee's recommendations on resilience against cyber-crimes be viewed. In the year 2018, the committee issued a somewhat comprehensive report on developing and testing the utility of resilience building practices in respect of market infrastructure.

1. Certain supervisory practices converge in some areas of governance, testing, information sharing between banks, regulators, and management of outsourcing arrangement. The differences in Banker to customer and Banker to Services (BCBS) member's legal framework and degree of digitization persist.
2. Cyber-risks pose growing and evolving unique challenges to institutions and supervisors that require dedicated attention and resources. The institutions are expected to see that they are secure by design.
3. Cyber-risk management—The mature IT and operational risk management practices are used to address cyber-risks and to comply with supervisory requirements for resilience.
4. Management models such as three lines of defense (3LD) for cyber-resilience are not clearly articulated across technical, business, and strategic decisions.
5. Workforce—There are severe shortages in the staff required for this work. There are naturally serious challenges before recruiters.
6. Testing, protection, and detection is gradually evolving and prevalent but the response and recovery practices are not keeping pace.
7. Incident management framework is not considered necessary by many but incidence response plans are a necessity.
8. Attempts at involving a standard metric are yet to emerge.
9. Most observed information sharing involve bank to bank exchange. Communication from banks to regulators do exist. The speed, lati-

tude, security, and fluidity of communication among country's central bankers is conspicuous by its absence. Actually, any cyber-incidence has cross-border jurisdiction and taking formal steps required for sharing the information should not be difficult at all.

10. A common approach to third party dependencies is yet to evolve.

We now give some detailed information in respect of the steps actually taken by banks and regulators in this behalf. It would be seen that the increase in the frequency, severity, and sophistication of cyber-incidents has led the authorities and institutions to take various steps. These include legislative, regulatory, and supervisory steps to increase cyber-resilience. These are initiated even at the global level. These are

- The G7 issued fundamental elements of cyber-security for the financial sector.
- In 2016, the committee on payments and market infrastructure issued guidelines on cyber-resilience for financial infrastructure.

Cyber-resilience is clearly defined as the ability of an organization to continue to carry out its mission by anticipating and adapting to cyber-threats and other relevant changes in the environment and by withstanding, continuing, and rapidly recovering from cyber-incidents. Bank of England has issued guidelines for suppliers who offer threat intelligence and penetration testing services and who wish to be involved in CBEST scheme. CBEST is now considered as the world's leading framework for intelligence-led penetration testing of systematically critical organizations who stand to benefit its trusted approach. Ethical security testers, certified threat intelligence managers, and even simulated attack managers come under these guidelines. Monetary authority of Singapore has developed specific training programs. Some central banks have developed mapping and classifying business services, supporting assets and services as a basis for building resilience. Institutions monitoring and surveillance of emerging threats including real time detection, ability to detect adversaries before they move between systems, and relevant continuity and control policies are also being developed. There are some penetration tests. The majority of directed penetration tests focus on regulatory institution's protective and detective attempts. Australia, Hong Kong, and Belgium have developed a post incident learning review. Information sharing in all these areas takes place but is restricted to a given country only. It does not take place amongst regulators.

Bank of England

BOE has taken far more critical steps to improve the preparedness of the entities supervised by it. The idea is to ensure continuity and operational resilience. In the event of major disruption, the objective would be:

- To keep retail and wholesale markets open and functioning. In case, there is a danger to financial stability, they may have to be closed
- Orderly return to trading by providing a single point of information effective channels of communication to ensure a coordinated response
- Relevant infrastructure provider
- Facilitating market initiatives

Operational Resilience

It Is the ability of firms and the financial system to absorb and adapt to shocks. Improving resilience is a major responsibility of the organizations.

The Bank's Financial Policy Committee looks at the cyber-resilience of the system. Banks prudential and regulations committee and financial market structure board focus on operational resilience of the firm.

The policy has thus three dimensions targeting the right things, build up resilience, and keep up to date with current threats to determine level of resilience required.

There is a review of technology for cyber-resilience a cyber-triage questionnaire and CBEST that led assurance testing of cyber-resilience. Because of the global nature of threats, the cooperation with international partners become necessary.

Lastly, organizations should respond to operational shocks through well-rehearsed contingency plans and incident response processes. To ensure that response plans work, H.M. Treasury, Bank of England, and FCA all act together and have a mechanism to conduct a response. National Cyber-Security Authority and National Crime Agency are also included. The responses are tested regularly, and even communication times are tested.

We conclude by highlighting the fact that the severity and sophistication of cyber-incidents have led to a number of initiatives being taken. These include legislative, regulatory, and supervisory steps to increase cyber-resilience. The matters are so important that G7 issued fundamental elements of Cyber-Security for the Financial Sector. The Finance Ministers and Governors of Central Banks issued a guidance on cyber-resilience on financial services infrastructure. The FBI has now constituted action teams and they are ready to assist in cyber-attack cases anywhere in the world.

- Cyber-action teams are ready to travel round the world at a moment's notice to assist in computer intrusion cases. They keep on gathering information and vital intelligence that helps us identifying cyber-crimes that are most dangerous to national security and economy.
- Close cooperation with defense, home land security, etc.
- New products, services, or initiatives.

CHAPTER 10

Human Resource Management

At the outset we would like to clarify that we are not attempting a DIY [Do it yourself] manual section. The chapter very broadly indicates the problems which the HR departments in a digital environment are likely to be faced with and very broadly look at the possible solutions. How to achieve these results would vary from organization to organization and would be determined by any number of factors.

For the sake of analytical convenience, the chapter is divided into three parts. In part 1, we would like to share our own personal experience in transforming a snail speed organization into one which moved at speeds unknown in seventy years of its annals. In part 2, we deal with the transformation of HR processes and how the organization is to be wedded to the digitization process and in part 3, we also touch on recruiting and retaining highly skilled personnel. The section also touches on termination of services of certain people, and the need for doing it in a manner that doesn't cause anxiety in the minds of existing staff.

Preparing for the Challenges Ahead

We refer to a bank which prided itself on being very careful about its policies, particularly lending and equally in its selection of people to work. Further, choice of places was very meticulously planned. Even the stationary required was prepared in a manner to be in consonance with a two- or three-year trajectory.

V. C. Joshi, *Digital Finance, Bits and Bytes*,
https://doi.org/10.1007/978-981-15-3431-7_10

In 1971, the sedate existence was hit by a tornado. The Government of the day nationalized the banks and soon thereafter issued orders to this bank to open some 175 new branches by the end of the financial year and a large number of these were to be located at rural centers and the remaining mainly at unbanked centers. The banks were instructed to lend funds to sectors to whom they had never lent any moneys whatsoever. They had been told to cover weaker and thin file customers. Mere tokenism would not have sufficed since quantitative targets were fixed. The first reaction among various groups of staff was that if these goals were achieved, not only the particular bank but also other institutions would lie in ruins.

However, to the dismay of the top management team, new senior executives were brought in and the message was that this was the time for all hands to be on the deck. People who were found wanting and/or had serious reservations about the policy implications were made aware that in case they failed, there was every possibility of their services being terminated. The first major change was that the sector was subjected to a public scrutiny. The newly created Manpower Planning section, with the author being the head of that section, got a taste of such public probing. The first advertisement for recruitment of clerical staff got an overwhelming response. In all, we received 300,000 applications. It was therefore decided that in view of the fact that we had to recruit only about 300 people, we would allow everyone to appear for an examination and scrutinize the applications of only those who were to be called for interview. This was a very logical step but the case went to the High Court of the state and only after the logic was explained to the judges, was the bank granted permission to proceed further. We must admit that it was a great sense of relief when the judgment was delivered. Soon thereafter, we were able to complete the induction of another 800 candidates to the officer's cadre. The induction of these bright youngsters brought in its wake problems never encountered before. They were highly qualified and yearned to shoulder responsibilities. They quickly grasped the modalities and also were effective in their dealings with the customers. The only difficulty was that they had aggressive career expectations. The author must indicate that many of the people selected then, ended their careers at the highest levels before retirement. In the immediate period after their appointment, they were keen on postings in far off places and had no qualms on being posted at rural branches where they had to put up with innumerable hardships.

Senior staff felt considerably threatened, were worried that these youngsters could soon overtake them and that there was every possibility that the seniors might be side tracked. In the immediate run, the seniors started giving adverse reports about the aggressive behavior and at the planning and development department we had to review and overrule these cases.

In addition, we also had to change our policies in respect of delegation of authorities and a number of procedures which were primarily tailored for a comparatively medium sized branch setup. These were not at all useful where we had branches where there was only one person to carry out activities or only two people to run the branch. Changes in procedures and policies could not be made very easily. A number of objections were raised and the division heads in the manpower planning sections were chastized by some executives on the ground that decisions were taken that could be detrimental to the health of the organization. Add to this, when memoranda from certain rural branches were received and where they had demanded that the manager should be provided with the cabin, so that the confidentiality of their meetings and discussions with the customers could be maintained.

Ordinarily, these appear to be very flimsy problems. In an organizational setup, sometimes resolution of even simple issues can lead to debates on wider questions of economics of business.

While we were tackling the cabin problems, we also had to build up training facilities at five or six major centers and had to deal with logistics problems of transporting staff from various places to the training centers, provide replacement for those who were on training, and had to be ready for the next batch as the courses were of seven to ten days duration. The training imparted was highly specific and useful for work in given sections.

We had therefore, to constitute committees to review many of the activities in a small region and also some of the board committees to deal with issues affecting working of the whole organization. The case in point pertains to the performance appraisal issues. In the first instance, we had to change the entire system of appraisals and had to bring in a great deal of information about the skills required for the work done, the functions that they were performing. Where would a junior officer have occasions to show his leadership qualities? Was it proper to assess managers working at very senior level of the organization for punctuality in attendance? This revision of appraisal systems led to very difficult HR problems.

Could we use appraisals for promotions and placements, and while considering placements should "Seniority" in service be given a go by? Could we have accelerated promotions? should we on a regular basis have a performance review and communicate the appraiser's views to the appraisee? After the board committee gave its reports, a policy in respect of all these problems did emerge and was accepted in a large measure by staff unions and associations. At this stage, we would like to comment on a revised version of "Management by Walking". We used to hold meetings on weekends and saw to it that questions small or big were duly answered and acted on. We realized that even a small change, could lead to a number of problems coming up. Further, it was also very clear that we as change agents were impatient but at the ground level changes take place rather slowly. The reason was that on the one hand, they had to carry on the activities while trying to absorb the changes that had to be made. Gradually, the message that you can't solve today's problem with yesterday's solutions reached a wider body of staff members who shared our enthusiasm.

The raison d'être for inclusion was to highlight the fact that mere introduction of a large number can disturb not merely personnel functions but a whole lot of settled practices. Add to it the change in technology and one realizes the enormity of the task.

SWOT Analysis

The task before any HR department starts with a review of its existing staff. A normal static review on as is where is basis comprises age, experience, qualifications, tasks completed and assignments undertaken. However, even a broad-brush picture would probably highlight major differences in the various groups making up the "Staff". It is seen that the younger generations are keen on technology uses [aptly characterized Digital Natives] while the millennials [described as Aliens] are those who have acquired the skills to adapt themselves but are slow to adapt since like the younger set are not born to it]. A ten-year old boy/girl would perhaps know more about mobile devices than his parents.

The younger generation recognizes its own contributions and seeks confirmation. They want rewards and even frequent feedback. They are not inhibited by the new gadgets or newer technology. In fact, they look forward to learning new things and would be unhappy if they did not have suitable opportunities. They yearn for an informal work place and are keen for a proper work–life balance.

Those in the age groups of fifty-five and above are perhaps planning to leave and would be happy if the status quo were maintained. Their ideas of benefits would revolve around health benefits in the post retirement phase. Perhaps some training to improve their prospects for part time assignments would be what they yearn for. Actually, if they could get some contract assignment in their present job with flexi hours of work, they would like to be considered for those. They would not be keen on disturbances shaking the boat.

The groups in the intermediate categories by and large are believers in hard work and would not resist changes if their own interests are not directly affected. They are also looking for promotions and would be saving for children's' education and other needs. They have mature perspectives and manage group relations well and more so if they happen to care for a relative. Further, they have greater loyalty toward the organization and would be sorry if the relationship were abruptly terminated. They would also be keen on training to ensure that they can work with the new technology with all the changes it brings about. The organizational ramifications are of importance to them and would like to see that their comfort zones are not unduly disturbed.

These characterizations are very generic and have to be looked at from an organizational context. In the "*older organizations*" efficiency and effectiveness would have the highest priority. Decision making is generally hierarchical and rules based and roles and titles or levels are predetermined. They are also likely to be basing their decisions on previous practices and rules. These naturally lead to being highly process based.

As against this, the new setups are organized for learning, innovations, and mainly customer impact oriented. They have agile network empowerment, fueled by collaboration and knowledge sharing. They have structure-based responsibilities which are clearly defined. But roles and or job titles change regularly and are based on projects they are assigned to. The teams are primarily focused on work projects. They have team and work responsibilities clearly defined. It would be seen that these are more for smooth group functioning and effective execution.

At this stage we would touch on another dimension as it touches on career building. In a structured environment it starts when you join and continues till you retire. In today's context, working with sales, manufacturing, law, and finance, updating of skills is a continuous requirement. Career is a journey of learning and progress depends on how soon you learn and develop. Organizations are shifting to flexible open career models that offer enriching assignments, projects, and experiences than a static career progression. Software engineers need to upgrade skills every twelve to eighteen months. Professionals in marketing, sales, manufacturing, law, and finance have similar demands.

They [HR departments] have to draw important lessons from such an analysis. No doubt they would have their own assessments about managements' attitude to tech investments and improvements. These [Organizations' approaches] could veer around their being leaders, followers, or just very cautious in their approach and particularly in adoption of new technology and consequent disruptions. They have to think way ahead and move toward convergence. The focus would be on defining and addressing tough problems which would make a real impact. Bring together people with diverse skills and build up teams that could solve the complex problems that are bound to come up.

Nontraditional skills are required because we are dealing with customer demands which are unprecedented. It would necessitate building new avenues for corporate learning, functions using their corporate training facilities and learning centers for collaboration and leadership development and cross-functional innovation. As people become more dynamic in their careers the need to build relationships and connectivity becomes integral to perform and to innovate.

Thus armed, the HR department can now look at the changes likely to be made. The technology scene and the broad contours are now sufficiently clear and even the likely options can be discerned. The human resources inputs and the steps required to build up the required strengths is the need of the hour. With the end so determined [no doubt, somewhat hazy] we turn to examine how far the tools so far used for *advertisements, interviews, selection, and salary* need to be modified or replaced.

Before proceeding further, we must take note and serious note of the fact that in spite of technology developments productivity has not risen and has perhaps remained static. This fact was very vividly brought out by Friedman in his book entitled *Thanks for Coming Late*, which shows that productivity improvements have not taken place for want of technology absorption. Perhaps this would be a priority item in an HR department's action plans.

It is, no doubt true that technology has a profound impact on organizational processes, and transformed the way organizations recruit, select, motivate, and retain employees. Two major factors namely talent management policies and technology would play a large part in this. Technology includes the applications of computer devices to collect data for business purpose. HRM is a system that allows manager's, applicant's, and employee's access to human resources and related information and transforms the way that organization recruits, selects, motivates, and retains employees. The primary goal is to recruit and retain talented work force. Qualified, diverse, and motivated pool is the need of the hour. Customer satisfaction and a search for innovative ways to achieve the same would foster innovation and would be a major factor in attracting talent.

Over a period of time various devices have been used to attract applicants and these range from passive one-way technologies [web-based ads], or forms of technology to enable applicants to apply online. Technology that includes machine learning and artificial intelligence can help HR organizations create differentiated and smart people experiences that people are familiar with in their personal lives. To be a leader in the digital HR transformation means to deliver a personal end-to-end candidates and employees hire to retire experience. Sustainable HR will take on an increasingly central role, as digital business forces the organization to evolve rapidly. Embracing sustainable HR can help the organizations to take the lead on enterprise motivation to attract top talent and avoid playing the catch-up during the next disruption phase.

The above is perhaps in the nature of aspiration and hope. Reality is much different. It is perhaps still caught up between the earlier ways of doing things and the current technology-based systems.

E Recruiting: Does it help organizations to increase the number of successful applicants? The real question is does it attract talented and diverse applications? In terms of response is it encouraging to have a number of highly qualified people/applicants? Unfortunately, no research data is readily available to give a categorical answer. We would however add that administrative costs go up with increased number of applicants. A study shows that along with the number of some talented people, a large proportion of job hoppers, with unfavorable background also come in. Older applicants who are women are few.

These practices are passive and do not lead to applicants asking questions, seeking clarifications, or communicating with organizational members. This process creates artificial distance between the organization and the applicants.

It is increasingly becoming customary to have interactive technologies. It does enhance personalization of E-recruiting. Social media, virtual reality, blogs, and even virtual job fairs where potential employees and employers can connect in a virtual environment. They can even use computer-based simulations. Chat rooms, webinars, and web casts to browse booths can all be useful in encouraging good applicants to post their bio-data/resumes. We have been asked about the flood of applications for jobs as assistants. We are not advocating time consuming processes for low skilled jobs. These are essentially for talent.

These employees want to be empowered and seek challenge. They enjoy teamwork and communities. They want continuous feedback. They want to play an active role in their own development and are "learning workers". They are committed to companies whose raison d'être they share. They mix personal and professional life, aren't loyal and dream of creating their own start-ups, and like to be empowered to get things done. They have an appetite for challenge and seek collaborative arrangements to achieve the desired results. They want to recognize communities of talent and expect their managers to give them immediate feedback; they would demand feedback and want responses or suggestions in every domain (performance, learning, career development, etc.) They don't understand the concept of career paths/layers and count on themselves to define their own development path. They value university degrees and higher education and see themselves more as "learning workers" than knowledge workers" and commit to company whose raison d'être they share. They aren't satisfied with current compensation models. They don't compartmentalize personal and professional life. The issue is no longer "work-life balance" but integrating the two. Most have worked at their current company less than three years and would like to create their own businesses. Some HR people even advocate crowd sourcing.

1. The next step is to select the candidate after scrutiny of his job knowledge, skills, and proven track record.
2. Should the organization hire the most talented people only? There are other considerations also and there are a whole lot of technology applications that can be handled by people who are knowledgeable but may not have excellent qualifications.
3. Job Analysis could lead to a proper understanding of the requirements and some jobs could be broken into suitable segments so that time required for completion would be much less.
4. Cognitive tests and personality tests could be administered on line and scrutiny about suitability can be completed.

We would also suggest that E-learning does provide greater flexibility, efficiency, convenience, and costs far lesser than a formal course would. The learner's perception about the utility of such a course for on-the-job applications is of great value. The content opportunities for practice and even use of tools like AR have shown to be of great practical value in complex jobs like fitting airplane parts. Even the trainees could finish them in record time.

Virtual simulations can be put to effective use when there are applications. In the financial services we are not using rocket science. Much of the requirements can be met through AI. It is proved that today's AI applications are somewhat simple.

Performance management through E-measurement techniques would show the employee's satisfaction levels and could be used for development and not for rewards.

At the organizational level, trained and experienced staff can be a very expensive proposition. Therefore, to take away biases in these matters organizations use compensation planning systems that reduce administrative costs and would be quite objective. It would be useful if organizations can have

- Automated payroll systems
- Design compensation systems and benefits
- Communication of such compensation systems individually

It might be useful to see to what extent the employees really value a salary package. It is observed that there are marked differences between millennial and GenY. Gen Y were keen on job security, relaxed work environment, and personal growth. E-Rewards is perhaps valued more.

The findings suggest that employees prefer more active, interpersonal, informal approach to all these areas of HR management. The technology is basically to expedite transactions. The implicit/explicit goal is not mere speed and efficiency but employee perception of organizational climate and culture and overall effectiveness of the organization.

Proposed Organizational Set-up

We now turn our attention to the organizational setup suitable for the digital environment. This is necessary because the grooming of our staff has to be in that direction. Their aggressive career expectations can be met if and only if they [no doubt, with organizational support] take steps for self-learning and widening their frontiers to cover wider management issues along with management of teams under their care, financial issues and inculcating organizational values. They have to break out of the narrow specialization and look on themselves as the future top management.

It is at this stage that their grooming becomes very important. We have seen that the former career path planning has ceased to be the guiding chart. One needs a new set of rules to reflect the shifts in mind-set and behavior necessary to lead, organize, motivate and manage and engage twenty first century workforce.

Technology is advancing at unprecedented rates. AI, Mobile platforms, sensors, and social collaboration have revolutionized the way we live, work, and communicate. Frankly, one does at times feel overwhelmed. With AI, Mobile platforms, sensors, and social collaboration, as pointed out earlier, being available, improvements in business productivity is of crucial importance. A proper coordination with public policy covering inequality in incomes, unemployment issues, immigration, and trade policies are all likely to affect businesses function and one needs to have sharp antennas.

We have felt that a tiered system does help to identify those who could be given a fast track promotion. In a big organization selected candidates may have aggressive expectations. But everyone cannot be groomed as a future top management candidate. The weeding could be through a process of project allocation and tasks therein. Those who show the abilities to complete tasks with proper budgetary controls and without adverse comments from observers regarding their interpersonal relations can be given due recognition and put under further scrutiny to see how they carry themselves in another situation, say a job that involves marketing products in a different and difficult market environment.

It is, no doubt, tempting to hazard a guess and make a ten cents worth of our own contribution. As organizations become digital, they face a growing imperative to redesign themselves, to move faster, and adapt more quickly. They have to facilitate rapid learning by the staff and only then would it be possible to meet the dynamic demands of their younger colleagues. Equally important is the way they carry themselves after they are promoted to the next ladder where they could meet any number of aggressive competitors. The tasks would be much more challenging, complex, and could at times be nerve racking. Maybe they have to deal with tough Union negotiator or some known difficult staff members.

These are the testing grounds and there could also be some odd characters supervising them. In financial services you do get some who have no time to teach their subordinates or expect them to be knowledgeable. Robert Rubin, in his autobiography *In An Uncertain World*, gives a few illustrations of how some of his Goldman Sachs seniors used to treat their assistants. It takes all to make the company's world. These people could be expert bond dealers. But they were not good man managers.

The first two/three years grooming should get the candidate to settle down. At this stage we would look at the digital environment to see if there are any changes necessary to the above overall analysis. The digital transformation is the realignment in technology, business models and value propositions. At the heart of it are people. Human capital is ultimately going to bring about

- Innovation[s]
- Soft-skills, creativity, innovation, and emotional intelligence.
- The possibility of using technological knowhow. The technical skills are the most important.

In such an environment a combination of high-level policy and grassroots improvisation has produced social benefits including easier and more widespread access to computers and information; increased scientific collaboration; economic growth; the formation of virtual communities and an increased ability to maintain social ties over long distances; the democratization of content creation; and online political and social activism. The Internet's rapid growth has also spawned technical crises, such as congestion and a scarcity of network addresses, and social dilemmas, including malicious and illegal activities and persistent digital divides based on income, location, age, gender, and education. Such problems continue to demand creative solutions from scientists, policy makers, and citizens.

HR has to clearly define its changing role. If it fails to adapt and get the teams to do so, the reorganization and disturbed work environment would lead to certain chaotic outcomes. We would touch on one aspect. The large Financial Institutions are able to draw well qualified candidates from good schools as the recruitment from Wall Street shows. This by itself provides an encouraging environment and the task of HR becomes more challenging. It must ensure that its governance practices are comparable to any other comparable entity. The end-user experience would speak volumes for the practices and their impact.

Learning and talent management

Effective participation

The challenges which they have to meet can be summed up as under:

1. FinTech as a driving model
2. The sharing economy will be the important predicator of growth
3. Digital becomes main stream

4. Customer reactions would be the most important guide for growth and profits
5. Cyber-risks and security will be a top risk.
6. Machines and humans must develop a symbiotic relationship
7. Regulators would be critically evaluating technology usage

It is in this environment HR would have to take the responsibility to provide the right people at the right time at a price which the balance sheet can bear.

In the situation described above HR functionaries will have to partner with various sections like IT, Marketing, and Internal Communications. They would have to have an agile approach to recruitment. They should guide and create an atmosphere of learning and even monitor employee learning. They should focus on collaborative work.

The use of chatbots and creating a digital coworker would be part of their work now. Finally they must learn to manage full time employees, consultants, free lancers, and part time employees. Nearly 30% of the employees are gig economy workers. The HR would need to have creative judgment and flexibility and try to see if some of the employees could have a long-time relationship.

We would conclude with a special section on training. The training would start with customer feedback sessions. The employees must learn to understand the importance of being trained to get the nuances and slightest hints from customers. Tweets, Facebook posts, and formal written complaints are all important sources for information gathering.

These need to be very carefully analyzed and remedied. Misunderstandings need to be cleared up as soon as possible. The customers are looking for seamless experience [s] and at every step of their journey it is the duty of the staff to ensure that it is what it professes to be.

1. Video training facilities for certified courses, and other training which could directly or indirectly help their career development
2. Wellness Management courses including fitness management, diet, wellness, health, behavior changes, and even travel time engagement
3. Social and community recognition, customer meets, anniversary events, etc. community service groups
4. Expert content on work and related activities
5. Analytics
6. Use in Planning, correlating people to business, predicting business.

We are aware that some of the suggestions would appear to be in the nature of Big Brother channelizing their life style. Far be from it. It is up to the employee to avail such facilities. HR department provides the infrastructure. In banks they have guest houses at various hill stations or seaside resorts. It is not obligatory to use them. Staff members are free to go to a hotel if they so desire.

The attempt is to ensure that efforts are made to retain the staff.

We would also like to touch on a more difficult task. Consequent to technology improvements, there would be a certain reduction in staff strengths. The process has to be handled very carefully. It might lead to a situation where certain resentment against technology improvement builds up. Lesser skilled workers find that their prospects outside are bleak.

A peculiar problem emerges. Welfare benefits, health insurance, and other concessions could well be tied up with the job. How do we ensure their continuation? One could be at a wrong age and have peculiar expenses like educational fees and expenses for college going children. There would be a need for a long-term solution to these problems. The days of boasting about terminations are gone. One needs to have a sensitive approach to a complex problem. Issuing pink slips is easy. Dealing with the impact on another person's life is difficult; more so when everybody would be watching and assessing as to what would happen if he were in the same situation.

Staff Strenght—Change Required

The perusal of the first two parts would bring home the need for going somewhat slowly, particularly when one has to keep the current activities going. The problem outwardly appears simple. It is not just an Issuance of a "pink slip". One will have to look at the impact on staff recently recruited or on those who have worked for the organization over the last few years. The HR department will have to consider the kind of difficulties the staff whose services are terminated would face. Health insurance, fees for the college going children, expenses of looking after a relative have to be met, and suddenly the employee finds himself totally stranded with nowhere else to go. Perhaps, suitable transition measures along with cushioning of hardships would be needed.

The induction of the new staff members and introduction of new system must be tailored to be in sync with organizational preparedness (maturity status).

Further, the "Why" of the changes must be made known. Every effort should be made to ensure that the staff and the management are on the same page. One can't forget that in spite of Financial Institutions having a huge database, they have had to depend on their staff for a number of items not documented. Much of it is in organizational memory. It is passed down whenever there is a change of guards.

Under such circumstances, a smooth transition can be ensured only when the staff also is involved. Very often, we tend to forget that we ourselves and our staff experience and see for ourselves as "Consumers" of what is on offer outside. They therefore are aware of the problems and keep on comparing what and how their own organization is performing. The FIs should not forget that this latent valuable feedback should be put to use.

HR, and other related departments like IT, Marketing, and such have a very important role of being conduits between the staff management and other functional departments. The top management should take advantage of the role the functional departments can play.

Then comes a very difficult task which the HR has to perform. They must work out the broad contours of the work of the future. It certainly is not going to be as simple as what the CEO of a German bank wanted. He is reported to have said that by installing 500 robots, he would run the bank without a single staff member. One can't forget that after the introduction of ATMs, number of tellers has not gone down. In fact, it has changed the nature and quantum of the work done. Counting and dispensing cash is no longer their main work. All that has undergone a change. To many of the customers, they are the "Bank".

Equally important, HR will have to be on the lookout for recruiting "skilled" staff for senior positions. One can't have situational advantages like being in or around Silicon Valley. The primary challenge would be to get them and thereafter to retain them. These days, the highly skilled and experienced staff is required in various departments and have to be treated equally well. Unfortunately, some of them may be more equal than the others. HR has to draw out its own priorities.

Outwardly, these tasks appear to be highly challenging and impossible to get done. Start doing them and solutions would be found. They are your today's problems and yesterday's solutions would not be of any use.

CHAPTER 11

E-Marketing

Digital Marketing

For the sake of clarity, we divide this discussion into two parts. In Section 1, we work out scenario on an "As If" basis. The idea is to present a picture that would emerge if and when we have fully digitized entities. In Section 2, we indicate how the bank(s) should gradually shift its brick-and-click marketing efforts so that over a period, it could be in sync with the digitization that is under way and that it slowly moves toward the digitization way and ultimately toward complete digitization from its present brick-and-click model.

Section 1

It is immediately clear to any observer that mobile "Apps" have overtaken bank's branches. Even the insurance sector is no exception to this change. Mobiles are used even to renew policies for the insurers and in short, it is getting to be the main method for interactions between the FIs and the customers.

We begin with an analysis of the impact of certain technologies that could have a dominant role in "Marketing". AI would be a major tool along with data analytics in the marketing process. Leads scoring and predictive analysis is a very important starting point for marketing activities. The FIs may have gotten some leads or inferred about customer's needs through their general comments or reactions. One may not be sure about

V. C. Joshi, *Digital Finance, Bits and Bytes*,
https://doi.org/10.1007/978-981-15-3431-7_11

converting them into sales. The application of AI would help in "Predicting" the probability of conversion into sales. The software could be used to initiate a dialog and the marketing department could try and gather both structured and unstructured data to get further insights into customer requirements. One could also have a hint about the potential competitors. At this stage, one could use emails to initiate an email dialog. The machines could continue these discussions as long as the marketing department thinks that it would give some results and stop before it becomes counter-productive.

The department could use different methods for establishing such contacts. The younger set would like to have contacts through Instagram or YouTube. The department could also provide online assistance to customers for completing and submitting documents and forms in case the department is planning to have more structured information. The main thrust for the marketing staff, should be on improving customer experience and engagement. We are aware that a major difficulty in working out solutions on these lines is the training of staff. The staff should accept the digitized working. We hope that we are right in assuming that at least some staff would be required and would be available. We are further assuming that due care would have been taken in initiating the transformation process.

It starts with a commitment on the part of management to move toward digitized working. It will be their responsibility to make training facilities available so that the staff can upgrade their skills. Needless to add that there must be an assurance and the firm belief in the objectives pursued at various levels. Lastly, the employees should have a role in the changed environment.

The changes in the work culture have to move at a certain fast pace. Companies do not have the luxury of trials and pilots. Silicon Valley, as Jamie Dimon, CEO of JPMC [JPMorgan Chase] puts it, is at the door. The exercise should begin with a clear enunciation of strategy. One has some guidance available through the work done by major companies like Gartner. They have taken a comprehensive view of the whole process and one could list the steps as under:

- Vision
- Strategy
- Processes
- Customer Experience

- Information and Insights
- Technology
- Metrics

The objective, simply put, is achieving a balance between customers' needs and the value for the organization (stakeholders). It would be necessary to start with an axiomatic statement that Customer Relation Management (CRM) is a business strategy and not a technology strategy. A further detailing of the strategy would show that the aim is to optimize the profitability, revenue, and customer satisfaction. The process must ultimately lead to customer satisfaction and the whole approach must be customer centric.

It must be stressed that CRM should be an enterprise-wide initiative. The whole organization should individually, and collectively, strive to develop a sense of loyalty for the product and ensure that they see value in it. The employees should appreciate that they have to pull various levers to achieve the customer satisfaction goal. It would be necessary to see that the various methods that are intended to be used are clearly spelt out and translated into action. "Authenticity" is of prime importance. The "Games" that people normally play, need to be forgotten. They would be harmful to everyone around. The stakes are pretty high.

The vision outlined above leads the FI to suggest and guide the customer toward the bank's offerings and/or to the use of bank's services. The idea would be to offer the service on demand. In the final analysis the customer must feel that his life has been made easier and qualitatively better with the acquisition/availing of a given service.

Section 2

We have seen in the earlier chapters how the FinTechs have disrupted the banking/insurance business model. In response to the change/changing environment, banks/FIs have also taken some very important steps to counter these threats. On the one hand, they are moving (though the steps are somewhat faltering) toward digitization and in addition have taken over a few FinTech companies which were available for grabs. Of course, absorbing these FinTech companies was not an easy exercise. They brought with them an innovative spirit and an aggressive approach to business development. To absorb these companies, in the banks' regulated environment and highly structured decision making was a complex and difficult task.

The digitization process normally begins with "Cloud Storage" and steps have to be taken to transfer data to cloud. The process is perhaps yet to start or could be underway. Further, a search for data analyst and staff required for innovation centers, experimenting with "Sand Boxes" should be on the priority list of HR departments. The banks/FIs are now almost ready for the quantum leap. After all, one can't initiate such changes in one go. It is not as simple as replacing typewriters with computers. The learning curve is quite steep. As planners, we would suggest that banks should start in a small way and could choose from one or two options detailed below. We are firmly of the view that the process should start at the branch level. To an extent, the choice of the option would be largely determined by the organization's plans and general level of maturity in the use of technology in operations.

In the first instance, with a technically mature bank, the decision would veer round to opening a bank like Alior [refer to Chap. 5]. It could be a stand-alone E-Bank with completely digitized features. It could even be modelled on the lines of an Apple Store with technology determining the kind of layout both for staff, customers, and required tools. Further, it could have departments between which customers interact frequently and they probably are required to switch from one to another (credit cards and payments).

The data analysis could be done by a branch to which such an E-bank is attached. The starting point could well be the borrowers/valued customers of the main branch. The reason for it is simple. We have their data readily available and we also know about their supply chain links and even these can be closely monitored and integrated with the analysis. Thirdly, the bank will have a fertile ground for experimenting. One could easily turn the bank into a clearing house for product sale. In a small way, we had carried out such an experiment, and 85 to 90% of customers of our zone found that the bank could virtually meet their requirements. The spares/raw material required by producers could be available through banks/or customers [producers, financed by the bank] customers/borrowers and could easily facilitate payments amongst themselves. The bank's website in a sense becomes a clearing house.

The branch space could easily be used for social networking and equally important for financial literacy. Great thrust should be placed upon getting reactions and spreading information about the way bank functions in changed circumstances. It could be an excellent opportunity for gauging customer reaction and more particularly in inducing a number of "thin-file" customers to visit the bank. It is likely that in many countries such customers shy away from the banks. The new teaching programs must rely on story-telling and demonstrations which would appear to be spontaneous and conducive to strengthening the get-together atmosphere.

The new teaching programs need to be spontaneous and the bank could experiment with a variety of publicity material ranging from videos and streaming information, to learning inputs. These "Groups" coming together could be used to gauge reaction to certain product offerings or bank's attempts at personalizing products. Such reactions may perhaps not be very specific or carry the same weight as those made after careful consideration. These must be looked on as "Banking Hours" spared by the customer for his/her banking transactions.

The banks could use such contacts for introduction of new products and it is likely that if one could succeed in turning these into "Happy Hours", one could get quite a bit of social media publicity.

Equally important would be the E-Bank for collecting deposits, making payments (national and international). Such a bank would be an excellent feeder for garnering deposits and execution of transactions for generating fee income business. It is here that FinTech companies could start developing apps for Open Banking or International Remittances. The contribution to fee income would be an indicator to the effectiveness of having an E-Bank as a subsidiary of the bank.

More important is the prevention of mistakes that might lead to serious cyber-breaches. Given the scale at which banks' activities are digitized, such breaches could be catastrophic. Equally valuable would be getting information on conversion of leads and customers sharing their thoughts, ideas on the marketing material mailed to them. One could ascertain if the customers found the material useful, very useful or not at all useful. The bank could get important guidance in deciding how long should AI driven emails be sent to customers. Every care must be taken to see that the messages are not counter-productive.

At the same time, the deposits should be transferable between the E-Bank and the branches of the bank. These should be interchangeable. The customer could get an advantage through higher interest rates and also have the benefit on the liquidity front. We have so far suggested a slow but steady step toward digitization. It might be useful to describe/depict the kind of branch we may have for the digital age. It is in the light of available technology development and perhaps borders on the ideal that one may think of. It starts by assuming that the branch is a required feature and that it is not going to be obsolete. Perhaps the digital technology holds the key to the branch of the future.

Most customers now carry the banks (smart phones) in their pockets. The smart branches therefore should be equipped with the following:

- Banks' staff with tablets
- Interactive Teller Machines (ITM)
- Video Conferencing Rooms
- Service Terminals/Kiosks
- Robot Greeters
- Interactive Digital Wallet

Interactive Teller Machines

The Interactive Teller Machines function as a bank in a box by incorporating human connection to a human banker. ITMs extend banking hours. The customer should do most of the things he planned to get done at the branch itself.

Service Terminals

These are simple, less expensive devices that can be placed either inside or outside the premises. They are of great value to a digitally less inclined customer. They could complete their own financial transactions like money transfer, application for new products, and offers/acceptance also through authentication devices.

Video Conference Rooms

The customers could get sophisticated advice and could complete difficult transaction like opening Letters of Credit and/or signing guarantees.

Interactive Screen Walls

Let us assume that a customer wants to buy a car from the car dealer. He taps on the wall in the dealer's rooms and lo and behold the customer is asked to tap on the car door. The car door opens and the customer is given a view from the driver seat. In the mean-time the bank is alerted. The bank immediately offers a car loan and then an alerted agent would be there to answer questions, if any.

We would, at this stage move ahead and suggest various alternatives for the banks to adapt when they launch a full-fledged program. We may suggest the kind of digital branches of the future as described below.

Smart branches would come in different sizes and appropriate technology devices like self-service areas for ATMs and ITMs, priority lounge, standing desks for discussion with staff.

1. *A Box Branch*: would be a fully digital booth. There would be secured entry for one customer. The total area would be less than 10 square meters. There would be 24 × 7 entrance and self-service terminals to meet the customer requirements.
2. *A Standard Branch*: would be a small branch with digital solutions and some assisted human interface. Slightly less than 140 square meters in size, they would work during standard hours and would offer in-person services.
3. *Segment Branch*: Apart from being digital would have Relationship Managers for specific segments. Standard hours for segment transactions and in-person servicing but 24 × 7 self-service.
4. *Flagship Branch*: Very spacious as large as 7,000 square meters. Standard hours for in-person servicing. All technology elements and all Segment Relation Managers.

It would be useful to understand the customer reactions to the changes proposed by us. In a sense, when customers evaluate the bank or financial institute, they do not evaluate a "Given Institute" but are comparing experiences. The answers received from the customers show that the customers want to complete the various tasks at the branch itself or a facility to complete the task as easily as possible.

The customers when questioned about the importance of physical branches answer that they would want a branch and more particularly:

- Access to Live person
- Arrangements for Fund Transfers, Bills Payments through online access

We must add that the use of mobile apps could perhaps change this perception. They would want to have most of the transactions over the Internet. They would like the simplification of process. The expected transformation of the banks is for simplification of designs, for removal of friction, and integration of new technologies.

One can't avoid the feeling that

- The bonds between the banks and the customer have weakened
- Technology induces new behavioral patterns
- Even the 45 to 60 age group now relies on mobiles.

True it is that even banks are taking steps to simplify their processes. The self-service design mostly evokes a favorable reaction. In fact, people now ask questions as to why go to a branch for self-service. Gen-Z would prefer some convenient physical location to handle the issues quickly. Self-service kiosks and bank lounges with some human interaction would be preferable to a branch visit. Interactive videos and components focus more on technology so that customers can do and learn more while at a lounge or center. Perhaps, light weight branches could spread services across a wider area. After all, interacting with someone face to face at a table in a lounge far exceeds the relatively impersonal interaction.

We could say that designing spaces and connections rather than sales are a primary change. But we can't forget that we are passing through a transition phase and that every effort must be made to maintain this delicate balance and move ahead.

We would now turn and see how industry analysts look at the future developments. In an article titled "7 Digital Marketing Trends for Banks in 2019", we came across the following observations which we think are of considerable importance.

- A great majority of consumers states that authenticity is an important factor when deciding what aspects to support.
- Voluntary content generated by fellow customer(s) catches our eye easily. Emphasis therefore should be on getting our customers to share their experiences.

An equally important part in meeting customer requirements is played by the way customers search for the required service. It would surprise many to learn that 3.5 billion searches on Google are voice searches. Curiously enough, personal assistants are playing an important role (Amazon's Alexa, Apple's Siri, Google's Assistant). Their capacity for recognizing human speech is increasing and that they are incredibly helpful. These voice searches give us quite a few results. It is estimated that by 2020, half of such queries will be voice queries and the answers would be offered by AI. In many cases, humans perhaps could not have answered them.

Chatbots are quicker than any human in any data related answer and in taking requests. They are now having personalities and even humor. WeChat is a very dominant mobile messaging app. It handles a bunch of shopping and other activities.

At this stage, it must be pointed out that customers are bombarded with messages which are not saved at all. What then comes into play is a micro moment response. I want to know or I want to do something are such micro moments. Consumers experience and act on micro moments at least 150 times a day. Marketers must remember that in many cases, these moments are important. There are four main game changing moments.

1. I want to know
2. I want to do
3. I want to buy
4. I want to go

We now enter the world of AR and VR. Our perception of reality is changing. In marketing general products, it is estimated that AR and VR would raise the total amounts collected through such demonstrations to be of the order of $200 billion.

Social media also plays a very important role. At the time of writing, 3.19 billion people are social media users.

We have deliberately highlighted such newer trends about customer behavior and would conclude that as policy guide the following may be useful. One could say that when designing and deciding marketing strategies, the following could be of great importance.

- Be authentic
- Make use of customer generated content,
- People do believe in their fellow customers
- Micro moments dominate the consumer journey
- Visual search technologies would perhaps provide new opportunities.

We are deliberately including a differently structured study (6 Ways to Improve Financial Content Marketing in 2019), where we found the following useful hints. There are a number of ways for developing marketing strategies in the times to come. It is necessary to look for useful hints from diverse sources. With the need to spread wide, we highlight the following. FIs and practitioners would, no doubt, follow what they consider feasible:

- Understand the needs of your potential customers
- Know your advantages and short comings
- Get the "Stage" in your prospect's mind
- Make your prospect decision easy
- Confirm your customer's wisdom

Despite the plethora of Financial Services companies, opportunities to establish a unique niche in the industry always exists. Analyze your market and target the prospect. Exploit the advantages and force your competitors to do battles on your chosen ground—the space in your customer's mind.

Preparing for the Quantum Leap

In what follows we now try to see how the click-and-brick strategy would be dovetailed in achieving the goal of digitization in the short run. No doubt, it can't be done overnight but the process though somewhat lengthy, can't be completed at snail's pace. At this stage, one would have to emphasize the existence of strong under currents, indicating a need for "human" contact. There is ultimately a need to develop a symbiotic relationship between robots and humans. Humans will have an important part to play in ensuring and enhancing not only the overall CRM policy but also in achieving corporate goals.

The speed with which the information is transmitted, stored, and analyzed would give rise to qualitative changes in marketing. Information dissemination and information-based decision making needs to be developed in various departments concerned. This period in the journey needs to be used to inculcate the value of information in facilitating the exchanges. The information has to travel within the value-added chain as given under:

1. Downstream between the firm and the consumer
2. Upstream between the firm and the FI
3. Within the firm itself

Once customer satisfaction becomes a paramount activity, the goal of dovetailing efforts to the development of practices, procedures, and processes would be an ongoing activity.

We have to take care of the existing customers (senior citizens, thin-file customers, and others) who are likely to need hand holding support even though they have shifted to mobile banking.

The staff will have to satisfy customers using mobile and Internet facilities and on the other attend to customers still using the branch network to meet their requirement needs. The staff will have to see that promises made and practices match. We are aware that in the post crisis period the customer service has suffered.

The customer feedback obtained through any means becomes a key element in the process. The organization must utilize the transitional phase to see how the consumer choices could be broadened. The consumers of intangible products can create their own combination of contents.

At this stage, the pricing of services would be a key element. The pricing decisions in the case of intangible products are no doubt difficult but their contribution to the income stream cannot be ignored. A very delicate balance has to be achieved.

Having invested substantial amounts in technology upgradation banks have to ensure that objectives are well achieved. It has to be asserted that successful strategies are built around customers. They have to evolve a framework that meets customer needs. Competing on prices and products would not be enough. The only tool available would be customer service, reliability, and trust.

A major stumbling block in persuading clients has been a lurking fear that these distribution channels are secure. The customers strongly believe that these channels are susceptible to crimes and that banks would try and pass the buck to the clients. Further they believe that the crimes are not localized and one faces great risks in using these services. We would not like to underestimate the dangers lurking in the Internet services. However, we must not exaggerate and avoid the use. There are such dangers even in paper transactions. Frauds, misuse of bank funds are somewhat inherent to the system. Banks must therefore educate not only their customers but even their staff members in the advantages of such use and educate the customers in the care to be taken while using these facilities. Merely having formal agreements which are primarily to safeguard the banks'/FIs' interests are of no avail. Marketing efforts in the initial stages will necessarily have to be concentrated on educating the customers. One is reminded of the days when rural customers had to be introduced to the banks and persuaded to use the services offered.

Despite the wealth of evidence that information and information technology are rapidly transforming almost all phases of economic and business activity, relatively little formal attention has been paid to the effects of transformation on marketing theory and practice. In the absence to date of a significant body of empirical work in the area by academics, most of what is known about information environment and marketing comes from rapidly accumulating evidence and documenting corporate experience.

Conventional marketing activities are transformed because World Wide Web presents fundamentally different activities than traditional media. The transformation takes place because traditional methods cannot easily be implemented. Non-verbal communication is deconstructed ("Smiley"). Once you include the consumer, the goal of marketing could move from satisfying customer needs to inclusion of an altruistic, cooperative goal of facilitating the development of the market itself.

Driven by traditional mass media models, "hit" and "visit" counting implicitly try to achieve mass audience levels since traditionally advertisement effectiveness can be tied to consumer response. The one too many models used in theory and practice of marketing has only limited utility. The web in course of time would change the consumer's role as receivers of marketing information and would allow them to be active participants.

The focus during the early stages of the electronic revolution has been squarely on technology. Discussions are centered on access devices, software vendors, hardware platforms, and specific joint ventures or platforms. One critical component has been overlooked namely the marketing of these products. One may complacently perhaps assume that the product would sell itself. This unfortunately may turn out to be wishful thinking. It should be mentioned that there is no consensus view concerning the most effective approaches for marketing electronic products and services. Most banks have hardly any experience (except perhaps ATMs.)

One could begin by identifying the nature of the problem. The biggest challenge is to provide the customers the breadth of choice they demand. The customer is now in the driver's seat. Refuse customer a loan today and he would find numerous others willing to provide the same. Charge them interest for being overdrawn and they would move to one that does not. The brick/click model requires a well-thought out marketing plan which would satisfy both the Internet customers and those wishing to avail of branch network. In fact, some or quite a few customers could be in both the categories. Equally daunting is the task of ensuring a service level to which Internet customers are accustomed. A mismatch between promises and practices/procedures could have serious consequences. For the last few years Banks/Financial Institutions have been so absorbed with their internal issues that customer service received short shrift. The industry's propensity to raise fees to boost noninterest income has not helped either.

Before proceeding further, we need to look at some fundamental changes that have been brought about. We have referred to market "architecture" earlier. We now turn our attention to "intangible" products. In the "intangible" economy exchange of information is not a byproduct but a central activity of financial markets. Information driven dynamics of modern financial markets needs to be thoroughly understood. Perhaps one needs to modify Toffler's three waves and state them as under.

In agricultural economy there was a relationship between man and nature or natural products. In the industrial economy the focus shifted to man and machines and machine-made products. The intangible economy is structured around relationships between man, ideas, and symbols. We live in a "weightless economy".

How does one comprehend the digital economy? One has to look at the demand and supply sides.

Demand for intangible artifacts and supply of intangible assets-brand, intellectual property, and human capital could help in understanding the nature of these "products". These intangible artifacts include, among other things, different forms of information, and communication, audio and visual media entertainment and leisure, and finance.

Normally these are joint products. A song is on the tape. Replication technology now makes it possible to have the same on CDs, videos, and so on. There are hardly any limits on the capacity. One could replicate and have as many tapes as one wants. Additionally, the same content may support a number of artifacts. The products are nondestructive or non-subtractive (Knowledge as the ancient seers put it increases through imparting.) The cost of sharing these is zero. The owner of an artifact cannot prevent/limit its consumption without paying. The earlier equation purchases equal consumption is no longer valid. The number of free riders routinely exceeds that of paying consumers probably by a factor of three or even more. Further the consumers create their own combination of content.

The most important fallout is that conventional pricing and transaction mechanisms largely tend to be inadequate. Economics of scale are determined by consumption and not by production capacity. There is a further problem regarding information. Prof. Stiglitz calls it "infinite regress". It is impossible to determine if it is worthwhile obtaining a given piece of information without having this information.

Earlier pricing of intangibles was based on support. The price of a book was determined by printing quality and thickness. Content can now be disassociated and priced separately. In financial services equity research is bundled into brokerage commission. The range of pricing is getting broader and more complex. Further, depending on the supplier–consumer relationship, different pricing arrangements can exist. Internet is really a fascinating laboratory for selling, sharing, and giving away. These thus vary from metered charges, fixed assessed charges, or charges for ancillary services.

On the supply side is the greatest importance attached to brand management. Apart from brands are intellectual property patents; trademarks are critical competitive weapons. Curiously enough these are not seen on the balance sheets. *Reuters* acknowledges that its balance sheet does not include such strains as its neutrality, its software, intellectual property, its global database and skilled workforce.

Products even though successful could be replaced or could coexist with otherwise what may be called "book store effect" *Reuters* have 20,000 pages of data on financial services though only 4/5 pages are used by most. Their value is determined from the total database.

In the industrial economy excess capacity leads to inefficiency and costs. In the intangible economy it is widespread, functional, and inexpensive. It is inexpensive because the key flows are information. Providing additional information flows is different from that of physical goods handling. The long-term trend is for an exponential progression mode and a dramatic fall in unit processing and transmission.

The intangible economy undermines traditional frontiers and distinctions. Sectoral boundaries are crumbling—telecommunications, informatics, and electronics are now overlapping. Time-honored distinctions between work/pleasure, home/workplace, and intermediate and financial goods are crumbling.

Lastly there is a momentous change in the relationship between suppliers and consumers. The end of information asymmetry has also come about. The customer knows as much about the products as the supplier. The customer is now in the driver's seat.

The traditional marketing approach largely derived its fundamentals from Prof. Porter's thesis. Prof. Porter argued that for organizations to succeed in a competitive landscape their strategy must fit their overall organizational objectives. Human resources, IT, and finance functions must support the overall organizational strategy to reach the desired objective. Any functional strategies that are inconsistent with the overall organizational strategies would be doomed to failure. The thesis is far more relevant today than in yesteryears.

Banks/Financial Institutions must make a beginning by involving the Marketing Departments right from the corporate plan stage to its final execution. It would be difficult to conceive how they could otherwise meet the customer expectations. Figure 11.1 illustrates the dependence between business policy and several aspects, including the Marketing Department.

We have repeatedly stated that "marketing" departments have to be closely integrated with the total working of a Financial Institution. The old rule that "make business responsible for marketing and marketing responsible for business" is more relevant than ever before.

The role of marketing is undergoing a change and it is for the top management of Financial Institutions to ensure that the creative juices flow and the gray cells work in the productive environment. This should not be looked on as platitudinous objective to be chanted from time to time in customer meets or executive conferences. The organization has to strain every nerve to achieve the given end.

This would necessitate an enterprise-wide operational efficiency. A call center operative who is not trained properly to handle queries or an E-mail, which is not answered in a given timeframe [maximum 4 hours], could mean the loss of a customer. Financial Institutions could ill afford to forget that retaining a customer is far more expensive than acquiring a new one. The ultimate aim for Financial Institutions has to be customer

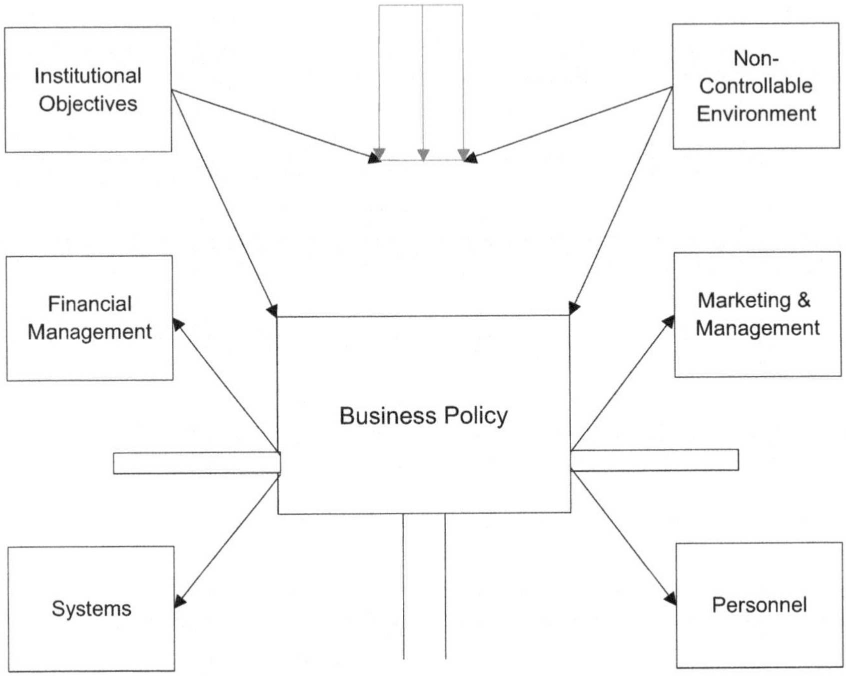

Fig. 11.1 Marketing plan in corporate plans. (Source: Author)

retention and more cost-effective marketing. Instead of advertising to a broad segment of customers many of whom would not find scattered shot sales pitches interesting, Financial Institutions, have to target specific customers deemed most likely to respond.

Donald Boudreace, Vice Chairman, Chase Manhattan Corporation, rightly says that customization technology is dynamite that is going to work. Thus, excitement must be tempered with a strong dose of reality. True it is that "market of one" is within reach. Financial Institutions can engage in electronic dialogues with online customers and formulate offers. A quick credit check, alerting customers regarding changes in interest or proposals to refinance when mortgage rates come down, are some of the ways in which a beginning could be made.

Nor should such things be left to marketing departments. In a "brick and Click" model a very systematic approach has to be adopted.

Marketing Objectives

This is an obvious starting point for marketing policy. A new critical dimension namely the need for "retaining" the customers have already been discussed. Along with this, the other objectives are, of course, as relevant as before.

- Profitability
- Providing high return on investment
- Achieving certain market share/growth
- Development of an image

To this list has to be added a new dimension customization technology and information infrastructure backed up by marketing strategy behind it. The challenge lies in delivering a customized message. Something distinctive and compelling to offer to individual customers. The "message" and not the medium would count henceforth.

Customization has to be viewed broadly. It has to be reviewed as one vital element in an overall customer value proposition, and therefore likely to meet with success. Obviously, such services have to be part of a package that includes other like online alerts, easy access, personalization of Web Pages tailored to meet personal interests are some of the ways in which customization would be appreciated.

We would once again reiterate the basics. Our experience leads us to believe that decisions re marketing are taken on an ad hoc basis like the launch of a credit card at a musical evening organized by a financial institute. Our contention is that such events have to be part of an overall plan.

Online surveys provide immediate feedback, but might annoy customers if they bear too much resemblance to the despised Internet Spam. The key in most cases is to weave queries into ordinary interactions between customers and the institution, so that feedback can be obtained with a minimum of distraction. Customers do not want to be bothered. The contacts have to be better leveraged. Additionally, feedback is important when the matter is fresh in the customer's mind.

The distinction between customers' planning their purchases through basic "research" and our guiding them cannot be glossed over. There is no rush to come out with product offerings. The customer is probably looking for a calculator or aggregated information.

This brings us to a critical review of the changing customer profile—skilled or otherwise, consumers could change their banks at the press of a button from the comfort of their homes. They will have access to aggregator web sites, which facilitate a comparison of terms and conditions. Further new players like tech companies are waiting in the wings with product offerings. Financial Institutions would be committing hara-kiri if they rely on customer inertia rather than allowing loyalty to stem from product features and excellence of service.

Financial Institutions will have to watch technological developments very carefully to see how the twin requirements of mass reach and security can be enmeshed. The other factor, which could tilt the scale from private to open networks, would be the need for different "products" to be available. Additional services would also be in demand.

The challenges before brick-and-click institutions emerging from "costing" of services are going to be a major strategic worry for them. The "marginal costs" of Internet services are far too low to warrant comparison with similar services offered at the branches. Branch closures and staff retrenchment could help in reducing overall costs but in no case could they bring down "transaction" costs. The service charges currently levied appear to be arbitrary and at no time does one get satisfactory explanation for the charges from the branch staff.

The charges for an ATM transaction could be a few paise while the same transaction at the branch premises could be several rupees. In one case customer would expect to receive benefits for the low cost of operations while in the other case customers will have to pay a hefty price for having the luxury of human interface. The hybrid marketing that would have to be resorted to can be demotivating for customers and staff.

Evaluation of Strategies

We now turn to marketing strategy evaluation. The results of any marketing plan must be reflected in the balance sheet and the profit and loss account. One need not wait till the information becomes available at the end of a year or in an unaudited form every quarter. Attainment of specific results is necessary to evaluate a given activity. We have noticed a tendency to substitute sincerity of efforts as a substitute for results. Sincerity cannot be an excuse for not achieving results.

Some departments function under a mistaken notion that they are not amenable to objective evaluation or audit. It is essential to dispel such a notion and subject "marketing" to a critical scrutiny not merely from an audit trail creation and adherence point of view but the review should look at:

Level of resources allotted. In case of net marketing they could be in millions. Some British banks had to spend sums varying from £ 145 million to £ 200 million. To create awareness sums of the order of £ 25 million had to be spent.

- Tactics and strategies used.
- Effectiveness and liaison with other departments.

Under such circumstances it would be futile to be under a mistaken notion that these departments deal with "intangibles" not amenable to evaluation.

At this stage it is necessary to refer to current research on marketing architecture and its impact on "marketing". We have earlier touched on it. Marketing executives and top managements must now ensure that they are attuned to perceive changes in these vital fields. Concepts such as "exchanges" etc. as pointed out earlier are assuming altogether new dimensions and do not mean what they used to stand for. In fact, marketing and support departments will have to focus significantly on increasing the productivity of their departments. Companies, which have successfully implemented CRM solutions, do report significant operational improvements, including revenue increases per person. Technology has to be leveraged to optimize sales.

Grievance Redressal

In today's systems, redressal of simple complaints like an error in a statement, an unaccountable change in balance, regular installment/standing instructions being missed result in complicated messages, mails, irritating conversations.

In times to come, call centers would try and sort it out. Before the customer presses the button, technology would allow agents to retrieve all records instantaneously in screen-pops instead of submitting written requests and waiting for weeks for all the documents to be assembled—the problems could be sorted out in minutes. The integrated data warehousing, telephony, and workflow technology should make it possible.

Market Turbulence

Customers need a human touch whenever markets are turbulent. The multi-channel strategy we have advocated above would stand the FIs in good stead.

In conclusion we would say that "ECRM" would enable the FIS/Banks to go to the heart of their customers' needs. These could help them to nurture loyal relationships, understand which customers and channels offer the greatest revenue potential and to cross-sell products more efficiently. It is the duty of these FIS to ensure that the relationships do not get completely depersonalized.

The main reason why these simple ideas are not translated into action seems to be that banks have not clearly entrusted the work to the branches. In a brick and click model the migration of customers to the Internet has to be undertaken by the branches. In fact, it has to be a profit center activity for them. Swedish banks have very successfully implemented such schemes and that the results are very satisfactory.

The second difficulty in our view is that banks are offering their customers more channels of communication but very little choice. These channels (particularly after the inroads that mobiles have made) need to be well integrated.

A customer's ID number should suffice not merely for access but also for enabling to complete transactions, share information with the bank, fix appointments, and so on. With back-office updates underway the bank could launch its portal. With a single events and customer file management were enhanced by an event and contact database that records interactions across the channels.

The magnitude of the task can be understood when we note that this meant integrating the data base of six million customers, with daily reporting of events and updating of profiles. This integration now has made it possible for the sales force to log in reminders of future intentions and make contacts positively at the right time. The bank is also able to develop a customer satisfaction scoring card. An electronic platform for bond dealing was the next to follow. Large bond dealing now gets done on the Internet. BNP Paribas has rightly claimed that the integrated multi-channel frame work has enabled them to manage almost 300 million contacts with their customers who chose their preferred channel for interactions with the bank.

The next obvious question relates to business results. Customers have seen a sharp all-round improvement in service. Each month telephone counters handle more than two million calls. Further planning for the sales team has become much easier. The customer relations service center now plays a more proactive role. Client files get enriched. And branch advisers are much better placed in handling matters. To our mind the most significant result is the realization by branch staff of their new proactive responsibilities for maintaining contact opportunities generated by the system. As Managers embrace this focus customer satisfaction is becoming the key performance metric.

The way ahead is known. It is for banks to ensure that the new mobile penetration (almost unprecedented scale) is taken advantage of. Banks/ Finance companies would be the losers if they fail to lose sight of the long-term growth prospects.

In the initial phases of the Internet era, there were a few banks (CITI, HSBC), which made a few services like viewing statements, broking services, or operation on the accounts available to via Internet to their customers. Discussions about marketing or modifications tended to be academic.

The last ten years saw dramatic changes not only in the increase in the number of service providers but also in the range of services offered via Internet. Further emergence of smart phones and their use by the customers has made financial service providers sit up and take note of the changes. The "marketing" of services has come to be recognized as a complex problem facing the industry, needing attention on a regular basis.

At this stage it is necessary to particularly draw the attention to a sizeable body of customers who are on the fringe of banking activities. They are having an account for the first time in their life. Going purely by anecdotal evidence these groups brought into the fold as part of an exercise for inclusive banking are being looked on as an unnecessary drain on the system. We are not at all convinced that this is a step in the right direction. Banks need to see if these groups would be the core group for their marketing efforts. These groups are the potential customers for micro lending and a number of other services digitally provided. They need hand holding support and the bank staff can surely do that work. The point of time approach to any customer development program can never be appropriate. It must be long range and spread over time.

We have in the earlier sections made it clear that hence forth the focus will have to be on widening the base and following Amartya Sen's capability improvement theme banks will have to be actively pursuing social goals. It might be useful to begin by reiterating the widened scope for CRM. It would be a business strategy with outcomes that optimize profitability revenue and customer satisfaction organized around customer segments, fostering customer satisfying behavior and implementing customer centric processes. Over a period, all three namely marketing, sales, and servicing are encompassed.

CRM in this changed context is, therefore, going to be an enterprise-wide initiative in which the enterprise would know how it wants to manage customer value and loyalty. Knowledge about how to pull all the relevant capabilities in place to achieve these goals remains rare. It would require a solid vision and strategy with supportive framework in the area of organizational collaboration, evaluation of customer experience, processes, information technology, and so on. We are repeatedly highlighting the organizational collaboration for the simple reason that marketing without such a wide goal fulfilling task would not achieve what it should rightly do.

Top Management should ensure that organizational bumps must not be allowed to hinder the smooth transition to a newer approach. One cannot forget that it is a do or die situation.

You have to be able to meet every customer wherever they want and through all the channels that are available to them. It would be pertinent to add here that these customers are not entirely unknown to the bankers. They have been on the radar screens for the last twenty-five years or so through NGOs, or other help groups working on the poverty alleviation programs or others running training programs or door step teaching groups, or through health camps. True it is that this was an indirect induction but banks/FIs did have direct encounters with these groups more particularly in rural areas.

We are now advocating a more direct approach since the costs of transactions and follow up would be considerably reduced through digital means. Let us not forget that inclusive banking programs have brought these customers in the FI's net and the FIs have to take up from there. Costs of getting new clients are and can be substantial. The fear is that FIs would lose them out to some who use FI funds but ultimate user owes allegiance to a different entity. FIs must aggressively move into these areas and deal directly with them.

How does one reach them? The first and most obvious answer is AI, Machine Learning, and Customer Analytics would be the driving forces. Cloud-based applications would go beyond replacing proprietary servers. New types of interconnected applications are possible. Platforms would be nimble enough to incorporate machine learning. Transaction tracking, handling rote aspects of transactions would make differentiation easy. In some recent discussions with expert groups, academics, and so on. we were asked to suggest how this could be done. Perhaps with a slight over simplification we would say that the following four steps should show us the way ahead.

- Assess IT operating model to determine much change it would entail
- Identify key pain points
- Articulate a vision for the future
- Identify 4–5 key initiatives

We must add that realigning IT in this manner will be no easy task. But the resulting agility and responsiveness is necessary to compete effectively against traditional rivals along with much nimbler fintech companies. These are the tools. What about the content? The first and obvious tool for "direct" contact is the mobile applications—the Apps! The mobile experience has to be closely watched and designed. With face recognition, biometrics, and so on authentication and entry should be much easier than before and should be a very smooth and unique experience. There has to be responsive design.

The marketing would entail designing a strategy based on

- Consumer Text messages
- Multimedia messages
- Geolocation marketing
- Mobile-centric tactics
- Facebook, Twitter—Community outreach, social events and philanthropic marketing
- Radio should not be forgotten and wherever possible the customer should be given a voice.

We now refer to content marketing. Writing, story-telling, editing, and publishing valuable content across channels would have to be resorted to. A distinction must be made between must-see content to attract customers. One needs to very carefully plan, create, post, and monitor content. It might be useful. This would be the marketer's mantra.

We now take a brief look at some other standard advertising methods. Paid ads are no doubt useful. Since these are getting to be very costly, they would have to be used sparingly and tailored very specifically. Data analytics should be used to enhance the specificity and content of such paid ads.

Video success story narration always has a demonstration effect and should be used specifically for the purpose. The problem is to get the audience interested and encouraged to stick around. Tools are currently used for educating customers in wealth management techniques with considerable effectiveness. We are proposing their use for different strata with a different message. CapitalOne has made considerable headway with its stories about "I am small business proud."

Customer Experience: Our attention to this particular area during a recent trip to USA when we accidentally got a chance to interact with some Airlines executives. They are watching day in and day out what their customers are saying. They have officers watching social media for customer feedback on each flight day and night. This writer was asked to define delays and when we stopped at two/or three they showed us that there are at any time six to ten areas which have to be under scanner.

The experience analysis is, as one senior marketing department executive put it, to find how enjoyable it is for a customer to do business with the bank or corporate entity. Trust is about the customer's ability to feel comfortable doing business with the company. Efficiency is about getting rid of the road blocks that potentially challenge the company's ability to provide service and instead prompt the customers to go somewhere else.

This is the experience era. The customers are vocal and aspire to be in the driving seat. Each day brings new technology and helps us in getting new experience. How the FIs approach initiatives that harness these trends varies. We can only say that ideas are often generated and conceptualized within teams that are dedicated to drive a seamless integrated experience. We have to have a sufficiently open culture to accept and absorb these.

We briefly indicate some technology driven advances to show how different institutions use these technologies to propel their business activities. ING has adopted an open banking solution that integrates a customer's accounts across various banking institutions. The customer can get an integrated picture and provides him with a dash board that:

- Instantly shows the customer available balances across all his accounts
- Predicts the monthly balance based on salary, spending habits and predictable debits
- Offers an actionable insight into available resource

Liberty Mutual uses Amazon's Alexa for providing customers access to get Insurance quotes (voice controlled) and answers other likely queries. Bank of America through chatbots and other digital assistants driven by AI, Predictive Analytics, and Cognitive messaging enables its twenty-one million customers using mobile apps to pay off, check balances, deposit checks, transfer money, and receiving personalized recommendations.

The tasks ahead are humongous. The thrust has to be on action. There is hardly any time left for thinking and re-thinking. The march of development technology cannot be stopped. The laggards would be thrown by the wayside.

CHAPTER 12

Regulating Banks and Insurance Companies

At this stage the regulatory aspects are in a melting pot. On the one side the US regulators are in the process of dismantling the frame and are keen on post crisis regulations acts/regulatory measures being done away with. On the other hand, in the UK, the trend is to have strict regulations and would consider ring-fencing a particular organization if so required. Additionally, through the financial conduct authority, they are using behavioral aspects to regulate certain practices which are considered not to be in the consumer interest and based on exploitation of some weakness in human nature being taken advantage of. We have, while analyzing the regulatory aspects relating to trading in securities, touched on the self-regulatory approach that is gradually becoming dysfunctional and giving rise to a possible evolution of a symbiotic system to evolve.

In the UK, some European countries and Australia, a parallel development is emerging with emphasis on customer behavior and what is aptly described as "nudging". We are not able to give a definitive and detailed analysis of the evolving mechanism. However, this should not be construed to mean that deviant behavior would be dealt with in a lenient manner. On the other hand, the regulators would come down heavily on these players who attempt to take advantage of some weaknesses in the human psyche. Further, even the law enforcement agencies also take a serious view of such events.

There would be stringent rules and the scope of regulation would be much wider. It should, at no time, be forgotten that these [Banks,

V. C. Joshi, *Digital Finance, Bits and Bytes*,
https://doi.org/10.1007/978-981-15-3431-7_12

Insurance companies] have a large Trust Deficit problem to deal with. Any laxity in this behalf would only aggravate the situation. We would briefly comment on an oft repeated complaint about regulatory compliance costs. They are high and compliance officers have considerable responsibilities in meeting the regulatory obligations. But against these problems one must take note of reputational risks. The social media and the various means for communication can cause considerable damage. We are constrained to say that the organizations should always have a crisis management committee ready to act as and when the situation so warrants. Even small matters which would impinge on reputational aspects need to be promptly and effectively dealt with.

We have noticed that many participants at our seminars confuse supervision with regulation and we begin by distinguishing between these two terms. Regulations generally deal with formation of rules that are on the one side part of the legislation and thus approved by national legislative bodies and on the other side rules that are implemented by administrative bodies. Contrary to this, supervision deals with the enforcement of such rules, either ex ante in the form of controls or ex post in the form of sanctions.

During the last few years it has become quite clear that regulating super markets in financial services is much more complex a task than is apparent. Added to it are the difficulties arising because the products are highly complex and have such obscure features that even senior executives of the organizations selling them are at time ignorant about the complex mathematics used. We were told by regulators that they too had difficulties in clearly understanding the risk aspects as also the circumventing of various rules for taxation. The regulatory agencies need to have a collaborative attitude in all these matters.

We have in our discussion of these aspects pertaining to securities trading and also cyber-crimes pointed out to an acute need for cooperation among regulators dealing with specific aspects pertaining to the financial services sector. The bankers and insurers can mount considerable pressure through their relations with legislators and others and the legislators must be equally alert to safeguard the consumers who can easily be victimized. We are (though some consider it an outmoded approach) votaries of the supervision with objectives approach. It is based on the idea that all the financial intermediaries and markets are subject to the control of more than one authority. Each authority would be responsible for a given set of objectives regardless of both, the legal forms of intermediation as well as the functions or activities they perform. Thus, there is not a great proliferation of control units. We are quite clear that this approach leads to a certain degree of multiplication of controls and can, therefore lead to a lack of controls. Being subject to the control of more than one authority might be more costly. But we are firmly of the view that costs need not deter us at this stage. The advantage of this approach is the requirement of the same rules being applied to each of the intermediaries despite the fact that they may fall into a different category from legal point of view. There is thus a scope for specialization and affords a solution to the regulation of complex and integrated advanced financial markets.

One sometimes is led to a conclusion that there should be a supra national authority for cross-border transactions for avoiding regulatory arbitrage advantage/disadvantage. Today after seeing the debacle of AIG, the need for such a body is keenly felt. The suitability of structures has been dealt with so far. However, the regulators will have to be alert about the system stability question. Equally important is the need for an efficient organization. In a global context the cost question assumes a great deal of importance. Further the turf wars that could emerge in such an organization could prove to be expensive from a systemic point of view.

The emergence of Crypto Currencies like Bitcoin (on a current reckoning there are thirteen such currencies) queers the pitch and complicates the problems. Initially we had expressed doubts about the acceptance of such currencies because of the adverse impact such developments would have on monetary policy if their acceptance were to be widespread. These apprehensions seem to be coming true, or at least moving in that direction. The fact that they are getting a worldwide acceptance is a matter of great concern. Further their operations are shrouded in secrecy and that sends a chill down the spine when looked at from the money laundering or moneys earned through unlawful activities like drugs. It is to be hoped that monetary authorities act in a concerted manner and control the genie before it devours the users.

Different regulatory approaches are being tried by different countries and one could comment on the efficacy of such measures by referring to the desired results. The model may be tailored to a country's specific requirements but the content is important. The regulators have to ensure the stability of the system. Equally important is the need to save ourselves from the rogue traders ruining us. How could we let greed and avarice overtake sound business practices? We could do it only if bankers were to constantly keep in mind that they are trustees. It is precisely for this reason that the Financial Institutions seem to have conveniently forgotten this cardinal principle governing their conduct that they are faced with a trust deficit problem.

We are of the view that the regulatory systems must be strengthened by bringing in auditors, technical experts, company secretaries, and that risk-based test reports must be made public. Management outlook on future developments, with the Board of Directors clearly stating what their appetite for risks is. It must come out every quarter. Further, even at the cost of being somewhat outlandish, one would not mind the Star Chamber methods for dealing with errant institutions. The Financial Institutions seem to be assuming that it is the duty of the state to save them, no matter, what they do. The bonus driven Financial Institutions should not assume the safety belt being thrown at them every time they show signs of going under.

We describe a model which has to perform the following basic functions. The present state of regulatory practices could best be described as being in a flux and emerging

- A provision of ways of clearing and settling payments in order to facilitate trade
- Provision of mechanism for the pooling of resources and for portfolio diversification
- Provision of ways for transferring economic resources and for portfolio diversification
- Diversification of economic resources through time across borders and among industries
- Provision of resources for managing risks
- Provision of ways for dealing with the incentive problems created when one party has the information that the other party does not have or when one party acts as agent for another

This reflects on market efficiencies and arises on account of information asymmetry. However, each type of financial service is regulated by a given authority independent of the operator who offers the service. The advantage of this approach is the requirement of the same rule being applied to intermediaries performing the same service though the operators may fall into different categories from a legal point of view. This approach certainly fosters economies of specialization within supervisory authorities and represents an attractive solution for the regulation of integrated and advanced financial markets.

We give below certain details regarding the way behavioral sciences inputs are being used for purposes of regulations. For the first time, the question of regulation is looked at from a consumer perspective. A casual look at the FIs product mix shows that many products are inherently complex for most of the consumers. In fact, many products involved tradeoffs between the present and future. Often people make decisions against their long-term interest because of self-control problems—excessive borrowing, using pay day loans.

Many of these decisions necessitate an assessment of risk and uncertainty. It is quite common for consumers to misjudge probabilities and make poor insurance or investment decisions.

It is often seen that such decisions are made on an emotional basis or some products as such do not permit any learning and correction of past mistakes. The regulators, therefore, try to identify biases affecting consumer financial decisions and either through guidance or the correction by the issuer, mistakes are rectified. The regulators analyze the following to understand the following:

- Preferences (what do the consumers want)
- Beliefs (what do the consumers believe in and the fact surrounding their situation and options)
- Decision Making (given the beliefs which options take us closest what the consumers need

Table 12.1 lists several behavioral biases and their effects.

We must also add that persuasion and social influences play an equally important role. In one sense if people are inconsistent it can be difficult to say that they are wrong. It should not happen that by preventing them from making such mistakes results in their being made worse off.

The focus now shifts to the biases and strategies of the firms offering products.

Firms obviously play a crucial role in shaping choices, product design, marketing, and/or sales processes. These can cause problems. Firms tend to increase non salient prices—credit card charges could be low in the beginning and higher at a later date. A classic example is the insurance contract where exclusions are never shown prominently.

Table 12.1 Behavioral biases and their effects

Preferences influenced by emotion.	Rule of thumb leading to incorrect beliefs.	Decisions made with short-cut methods.
Present biases reflected through credit card purchases. Immediate gratification.	Excessive belief in one's ability e.g. picking of stocks.	Over stating value of a packaged product and limited attention to future sales possibilities.
Reference dependence and loss aversion.	Over extrapolation over a few years of investment returns.	Mental accounting of investment decisions on a single asset and ignore total portfolio.
Regret and other emotions. Buying insurance for peace of mind.	Projecting bias taking loans without considering repayment difficulties in the future.	Investment splitting equally in all schemes.

Source: Financial Conduct authority U.K. https://www.fca.org.uk/publication/occasional-papers/occasional-paper-1.pdf

Table 12.2 Regulators answers to problems

Identify and prioritize risks to consumers	How to spot risks particularly detrimental and caused by bias? How can we prioritize risk?
Understand root causes of problems	Is consumer choice reasonable? Are consumers biased? What do they need? Can we analyze specific issues and market wide issues?
Designing effective intervention	Availability of intervention methods. Is intervention necessary? Assess impact of intervention.

Source: Financial Conduct Authority FCA Occasional Paper No.1 Applying Behavioral Economics at the financial conduct authority April 2013. https://www.fca.org.uk/publication/occasional-papers/occasional-paper-1.pdf

Of course, firms may not do all this knowingly. Bias exploitation may be the only way to attract and retain customers. The regulators therefore answer some of these problems in the following way (Table 12.2):

We now present below a detailed analysis of the points made above.

1. It would be easily seen that biases are rarely observable. Regulators need a set of indicators that help identify where consumer behavior

and the firm's response get reflected in the product feature. A right way perhaps would be to identify the economic function of a product and see if the consumer uses it for that purpose.

2. We need to develop a possible explanation as to the underlying causes and then fathom the buried evidence. Find out if consumers are making mistakes and if so, which biases caused them. The regulators need to get details about consumer awareness, essential products, consumer choices in different settings and the consumer's, self-proclaimed needs and objective[s].

   In this context we have to analyze firm's specific behavior. Behavioral insights can bring out what kind of dialogue to have with the firm and also what information to gather from them. Perhaps qualitative information and customer behavior may also be required. In fact, the following issues do require a critical examination.

   - Collecting firsthand information and data through consumer research.
   - Randomize controlled trials.
   - Analyzing broad context of the market.
   - Nature of present competition.
   - Market failures, if any and equally important regulatory failures.

3. Behavioral economics offers new perspective that financial conduct authorities could use. The interventions are ordered from the least to most and the following four ways are available to handle some of the behavioral problems noticed above.

   - Require firms to provide more information in a specific way.
   - Change the choice environment.
   - Ban specific product features.
   - Control product distribution.

We conclude on a note highlighting that doctrinaire approaches based on belief in market efficiencies must not blind us into adopting policies which are not conducive to the present situation. The ground realities warrant right responses.

CHAPTER 13

The Road Ahead: Alternative Model Digitization and Required Developments

This chapter attempts consolidation of different ideas scattered over different chapters into a cohesive whole.

In this chapter, we present an alternative approach for dealing with the digitization process (response to technology development and disruption issues). The "Solutions" and policy prescriptions offered by us and the suggested methods for achieving desired results are extremely difficult to implement. When implemented, within the organization which is moving and forced to work at two distinct levels.

The current scenario starts with a legacy system, rightly described as a spaghetti system and trying to make drastic changes thereto. At the organization level, one has a structured hierarchical system on which we would have to superimpose with a highly flexible one where the newly recruited staff members entrusted with the task have different needs and aspirations regarding their career development and even about their performance. Instead of a hire-to-retire policy, the staff coming in to handle the digitization process do not look beyond a short span before them. The same thing happens in developing marketing strategy. The resulting scene (chaotic is the only word that aptly describes it) naturally causes a great concern at the top management level. One can't ever think of a harmonious development plan emerging.

The planning department, no doubt, immediately sees the chaos that would emerge. The solutions to dealing with these issues could range from management team juggling a number of colored balls like the magicians of the past.

V. C. Joshi, *Digital Finance, Bits and Bytes*,
https://doi.org/10.1007/978-981-15-3431-7_13

Try and run parallel systems in the HR department. The HR would need to "handle" data analysts, young technically savvy staff members, while in the same breath deal with retrenchment problems in an otherwise stable backbone of executives. They would in the same breath have to persuade a person with three to five years of service experience wanting a raise in salary and at the same time threatening to leave in case the requests were not met. One could therefore easily appreciate the fact that a number of senior executives when questioned about their perception of risk have expressed the view that "Management of Change" is risk number one (Banana Skins for Insurance—2017).

Obviously, one would be driven to the search for other ways of dealing with these innumerable problems. Instead of trying to work out solutions in a "Complex" and what outwardly looks like an impossible situation, try to look for solutions.

The answer which we have been propagating for the last couple of years suggests building up either a full-fledged E-Branch/Bank right from design and layout for electrical wirings to architecture, it would be a different entity—main thrust of its work would be on being an experimental hub and an innovation center for a parent organization. The advantages in terms of implementation (away from the accepted beaten track) diverse policies may be appropriate for the digitized entity. These policies would be considered as proper and would not cause any difficulties.

The parent organization could use such a bank to deal not only with tech savvy but high net worth individuals but would help the parent organization in its socially desirable inclusive banking efforts.

It would in the case of the first group, provide them not merely the technology solutions but also with an app store like lounge with chatbot and, if desired, with a relation manager.

At the other end, "thin file" customers, would have facilities for financial training, guidance on their small business activities, and help in coordination with various agencies. For them, suitable technical support and assurances could be offered for executing their money transfer requirements. They would also receive guidance for suitable health insurance and this would help them in coping with the problem without reducing consumption or withdrawing children from school. Lastly, testing of AI solutions with emphasis on the improvement of systems, developing of measures for security checks and also less costly solutions for compliance of regulatory requirements. They would in fact, be expected to provide today's solutions for today's problems.

References

Accenture. (2019). Ninth Annual Cost of Cyber Crime Study. Retrieved from https://www.accenture.com/us-en/insights/security/cost-cybercrime-study.

Alzetta, F. (2019). 7 Trends and Tech to Watch. *The Fintech Times*. Retrieved from https://thefintechtimes.com/7-trends-and-tech-to-watch/.

Anguilla Financial Services Commission. (2014). Guidelines on Risk Management of Electronic Banking. Retrieved from https://www.fsc.org.ai/documents/Document%20Library/Guidelines/Guidelines%20on%20Risk%20Management%20of%20Electronic%20Banking.pdf.

Anticipating Disruption in Financial Services: CIO Journal. (2016). Retrieved from https://deloitte.wsj.com/cio/2016/02/17/anticipating-disruption-in-financial-services/.

Automation Your Friendly Neighborhood Branch May Go. Retrieved from https://economictimes.indiatimes.com/industry/healthcare/biotech.

Bank of International Settlement. (2003). Basel Committee on Banking Supervision. Risk Management Principles for Electronic Banking. Retrieved from https://www.bis.org/publ/bcbs98.pdf.

Beyer, M., & Laney, D. (2012). The Importance of 'Big Data': A Definition. Retrieved from https://www.gartner.com/en/documents/2057415/the-importance-of-big-data-a-definition.

Bhimani, A. (2015). Exploring Big Data's Strategic Consequences. Retrieved from https://journals.sagepub.com/doi/abs/10.1057/jit.2014.29.

Blake, M. (2018). 4 Ways to Disrupt Insurance with Customer Technology. *Forbes*. Retrieved from https://www.forbes.com/sites/blakemorgan/2018/05/02/4-ways-to-disrupt-insurance-with-customer-technology/#5ff0532382ef.

V. C. Joshi, *Digital Finance, Bits and Bytes*,
https://doi.org/10.1007/978-981-15-3431-7_11

Bloom, A. (1987). *The Closing of the American Mind—How Higher Education has Failed Democracy and Impoverished the Souls of Today's Students.* Simon and Schuster. Retrieved from https://archive.org/details/AllanDavidBloomTheClosingOfTheAmericanMindSimonSchusterTrade1987.

Bommel, E. van, Edleman, D., & Ungerman, K. (2014). Digitizing the Consumer Decision Journey. *McKinsey*. Retrieved from https://www.mckinsey.com/business-functions/marketing-and-sales/our-insights/digitizing-the-consumer-decision-journey.

Bradner, S. O., & Mankin, A. (1995). *Ipng: Internet Protocol Next Generation.* Addison-Wesley Professional. Retrieved from https://www.pearson.com/us/higher-education/program/Bradner-I-Png-Internet-Protocol-Next-Generation-Internet-Protocol-Next-Generation/PGM177533.html.

Christensen, C. M., & Bower, J. L. (1995). Disruptive Technologies: Catching the Wave. *Harvard Business Review*. Retrieved from https://hbr.org/1995/01/disruptive-technologies-catching-the-wave.

Christensen, C. M., Raynor, M. E., & McDonald, R. (2015). What Is Disruptive Innovation? *Harvard Business Review*. Retrieved from https://hbr.org/2015/12/what-is-disruptive-innovation.

Côrte-Real, N., Oliveira, T., & Ruivo, P. (2017). Assessing Business Value of Big Data Analytics in European Firms. Retrieved from https://ideas.repec.org/a/eee/jbrese/v70y2017icp379-390.html.

Cyber Law, IT Act Overview. Retrieved from https://www.tutorialspoint.com/information_security_cyber_law/introduction.htm.

Debnath, K. (2016). *Community Based Health Insurance.* Dada Purav Research and Training Institute, Pune.

Deloitte. (2018). Banking & Capital Markets. Retrieved from https://www2.deloitte.com/ug/en/pages/financial-services/topics/banking-capital-markets.html.

Deloitte Global. (2016). Anticipating Disruption in Financial Services. Retrieved from https://deloitte.wsj.com/cio/2016/02/17/anticipating-disruption-in-financial-services/.

Dijcks, J.-P. "Oracle: Big Data for the Enterprise." [White paper]. Oracle Corp. Retrieved from http://www.oracle.com/us/products/database/big-data-for-enterprise-519135.pdf.

Dutta, D., & Bose, I. (2014). Managing a Big Data Project: The Case of Ramco Cements Limited. Retrieved from https://www.sciencedirect.com/science/article/pii/S0925527314004265.

Ernst and Young. (2016). Customer Trust: Without It, You're Just Another Bank. Retrieved from https://www.ey.com/gl/en/industries/financial-services/banking%2D%2D-capital-markets/ey-trust-without-it-youre-just-another-bank.

Ernst and Young. (2018a). Global Banking Outlook 2018. Retrieved from https://www.ey.com/Publication/vwLUAssets/ey-global-banking-outlook-2018/$File/ey-global-banking-outlook-2018.pdf.

Ernst and Young. (2018b). The Revised Payment Services Directive (PSD2). Retrieved from https://www.ey.com/Publication/vwLUAssets/Regulatory_agenda_updates_PSDII_Luxembourg/$FILE/Regulatory%20agenda%20updates_PSDII_Lux.pdf.

European Banking Authority. (2017). Risk Assessment of the European Banking System. Retrieved from https://eba.europa.eu/documents/10180/2037825/Risk+Assessment+Report+-+November+2017.pdf.

EVERFI. Top 7 Digital Marketing Trends for Banks in 2020. Retrieved from https://everfi.com/insights/blog/digital-marketing-trends-for-banks/.

FFIEC. Cyber Security Table. Retrieved from https://www.ffiec.gov/pdf/cybersecurity/FFIEC_CAT_May_2017.pdf.

Financial Conduct Authority (FCA). (2017). Strategic Review of Retail Banking Business Models: Purpose and Scope. Retrieved from https://www.fca.org.uk/publication/multi-firm-reviews/strategic-review-retail-banking-business-models-scope.pdf.

Financial Stability Board. (2017). Assessment of Financial Stability. Retrieved from https://www.financialresearch.gov/financial-stability-reports/files/OFR_2017_FSR_Ch2.pdf.

Franklin, D. (2017). Megatech: Technology in 2050. *The Economist*. Retrieved from https://shop.economist.com/products/megatech.

Frey, C. B., & Osborne, M. A. (2013a). The Future of Employment: How Susceptible Are Job to Computerization. Retrieved from https://www.oxford-martin.ox.ac.uk/downloads/academic/future-of-employment.pdf.

Frey, C. B., & Osborne, M. A. (2013b). The Future of Employment: How Susceptible Are Jobs to Computerization? Retrieved from https://www.oxford-martin.ox.ac.uk/downloads/academic/The_Future_of_Employment.pdf.

Friedman, T. L. (2016). Thank You for Being Late. *Publishers Weekly*.

Gozman, D., Liebenau, J., & Mangan, J. (2018). The Innovation Mechanisms of Fintech Start-Ups: Insights from Swift's Innotribe Competition. *Journal of Management Information Systems, 35*(1), 145–179.

Griffiths, J. (2018). How Technology Is Influencing the Insurance Industry. Retrieved from https://www.technologyrecord.com/Article/how-technology-is-influencing-the-insurance-industry-62732.

H.M.G. Security Policy Framework Minimum Security Standard. (2018). Retrieved from https://www.history.org.uk/files/download/7311/1294317994/SecurityPolicyFramework.pdf.

IT Examination Handbook. (2016). Appendix E—Mobile Financial Services. Retrieved from https://ithandbook.ffiec.gov/it-booklets/retail-payment-systems/appendix-e-mobile-financial-services.aspx.

Joshi, V. C. (1972). *Manpower Planning in Commercial Banks*. Mumbai: Commerce Research Bureau.

KPMG. (2017). Top Ten Regulatory Challenges. Retrieved from https://assets.kpmg/content/dam/kpmg/au/pdf/2017/banking-capital-markets-regulatory-challenges-2017.pdf.

Kuhn, T. S. (1962). *The Structure of Scientific Revolution*. International Encyclopedia of United Science. Retrieved from https://projektintegracija.pravo.hr/_download/repository/Kuhn_Structure_of_Scientific_Revolutions.pdf.

Kuhn, T. S. (1996). *The Structure of Scientific Resolutions*. University of Chicago Press. Retrieved from https://archive.org/details/ThomasS.KuhnTheStructureOfScientificRevolutions/.

Markoff, J. (May 18, 1998). Long Before Microsoft's Internet War: A Peaceful Ethernet. *New York Times*. Retrieved from https://www.nytimes.com/1998/05/18/business/long-before-microsoft-s-internet-war-a-peaceful-ethernet.html.

Marous, J. The State of Finance Marketing: Adoption of Martech Solutions Remains Anemic. Retrieved from https://thefinancialbrand.com/73215/financial-marketing-banking-martech-technology-trends/.

McKinsey. (2016). Block Chain in Insurance—Opportunity or Threat? Retrieved from https://www.mckinsey.com/~/media/McKinsey/Industries/Financial%20Services/Our%20Insights/Blockchain%20in%20insurance%20opportunity%20or%20threat/Blockchain-in-insurance-opportunity-or-threat.ashx.

National Association of Insurance Commissioners. (2019). Data, Innovation & Cyber. Retrieved from https://www.naic.org/cipr_topics/topic_cyber_risk.htm.

Nawijn, B. (2018). 9 Applications of AR and VR in the Financial Industry. Retrieved from https://www.tjip.com/en/publications/9-applications-of-ar-vr-in-the-financial-industry.

Nelson, S. (2003). Eight Building Blocks of CRM. Retrieved from https://www.csoonline.com/article/2116935/the-eight-building-blocks-of-crm.html.

Organisation for Economic Co-operation and Development. (2016). Paper on Economic and Social Benefits of Internet Openness. No. 257. Retrieved from https://www.oecd.org/officialdocuments/publicdisplaydocumentpdf/?cote=DSTI/ICCP(2015)17/FINAL&docLanguage=En.

Porter, M. E., & Hepplemann, J. E. (2017). A Manager's Guide to Augmented Reality. *Harvard Business Review*. Retrieved from https://hbr.org/2017/11/a-managers-guide-to-augmented-reality.

PricewaterhouseCooper (PwC). Artificial Intelligence and Digital Labor in Financial Services. Retrieved from http://download.pwc.com/us/financial-services/lookbook/artificial-intelligence.html.

PwC. (2017a). Insurance Baba Skins: The C.F.S.I. Survey of the Risks Facing Insurance. Retrieved from https://www.pwc.com/gx/en/insurance/assets/csfi-insurance-banana-skins-web-2017.pdf.

PwC. (2017b). CFIS Insurance Banana Skins. Retrieved from https://www.pwc.com/gx/en/insurance/assets/csfi-insurance-banana-skins-web-2017.pdf.

Quarles, R. K. (2019). The Financial Stability Board in 2019. In *A Speech at the Joint Conference of the European Central Bank and the Journal of Money, Credit, and Banking*, Frankfurt, Germany, March 28, 2019. Retrieved from https://ideas.repec.org/p/fip/fedgsq/1048.html.

Raptis, S. (2013). Analyzing Cyber Risk Coverage. Retrieved from https://riskandinsurance.com/analyzing-cyber-risk-coverage/.

Rea, S. (2017). Information Avoidance: How People Select Their Own Reality. *Carnegie Mellon University*. Retrieved from https://www.cmu.edu/news/stories/archives/2017/march/information-avoidance.html.

Rifkin, J. (2013). *The Third Industrial Revolution: How Lateral Power Is Transforming Energy, the Economy, and the World* [Paperback]. Palgrave Macmillan.

Rinaldi, C. (2015). Fifteen Digital Strategies for Financial Marketers in 2015. Retrieved from https://thefinancialbrand.com/49927/digital-marketing-strategies-for-banks-credit-unions/.

SAS. (2018). G.D.P.R. Compliance in a Data Driven World. Insights from a 2018 Survey. Retrieved from https://www.sas.com/content/dam/SAS/en_us/doc/whitepaper1/gdpr-compliance-109048.pdf.

Schiller, D. (2000). *Digital Capitalism: Networking the Global Market System* [Paperback]. Cambridge, MA: The MIT Press.

Schiller, D. (2011). Power Under Pressure—Digital Capitalism in Crisis. *International Journal of Communication, 5*, 924–941. Retrieved from https://ijoc.org/index.php/ijoc/article/viewFile/1226/577.

Schmidt, E. Quote—The Internet—Engine for Change. Retrieved from https://www.goodreads.com/quotes/259999-the-internet-is-the-first-thing-that-humanity-has-built.

Shridhar, L. (2002). Cyber Crimes and the Real World. Retrieved from https://www.boloji.com/articles/6185/cyber-crimesand-the-real-world.

Singh, P. (2017). Financial Services Marketing Targets One and Not All on the Digital World. Retrieved from https://www.scmp.com/business/banking-finance/article/2124479/financial-services-marketing-targets-one-and-not-all.

Smith, M. A. (2017). Auditing Block Chain in Financial Services. *PwC*. Retrieved from https://www.pwc.com/us/en/industries/financial-services/research-institute/blog/blockchain-audit-a-michael-smith.html.

Snyman, J. (2019). How Technology Is Changing Insurance. Retrieved from https://compareguru.co.za/news/technology-will-change-insurance-forever/.

Stein, K. M. (2017). Lighting Our Capital Markets. *US Securities and Exchange Commission*. Retrieved from https://www.sec.gov/news/speech/stein-lighting-our-capital-markets-071117.

Stone, D., Lukaszewski, K., Deadrick, D. L., & Johnson, R. D. (June 2015). Influence of Technology on the Future of Human Resource Management. *Human Resource Management Review, 25*(2), 216–231.

The Economist Intelligence Unit. Whose Customers Are You? The Reality of Digital Banking. Retrieved from https://perspectives.eiu.com/sites/default/files/Global%20Retail%20Banking%20%282%29.pdf.

The Financial Brand. (2017). Will Augmented and Virtual Reality Replace the Bank Branch? Retrieved from https://thefinancialbrand.com/65828/.

The SWIFT Institute. (2017). The Role of Big Data in Governance. Retrieved from https://swiftinstitute.org/research/the-role-of-big-data-in-governance/.

Tzu, S. The Art of War. Retrieved from https://suntzusaid.com/.

U.S. Securities and Exchange Commission. SEC Charges Investment Adviser With Failing to Adopt Proper Cybersecurity Policies and Procedures Prior To Breach. September 22, 2015. Retrieved from https://www.sec.gov/news/pressrelease/2015-202.html.

U.S. Supreme Court Ruling [Reno v. American Civil Liberties Union No. 96-511]. (1997). Retrieved from https://www.aclu.org/legal-document/supreme-court-decision-reno-v-aclu-et-al.

United Nations Development Programme, Human Development Reports. (2007). Trends in Digital Divide. Retrieved from http://hdr.undp.org/en/content/trends-digital-divide.

United States. Cong. Senate. Committee on Armed Services. *Worldwide Threat Assessment. May 6, 2018.* 116th Congress. 2nd sess. Washington: GPO, 2018 (statement of Lt. Gen. Robert Ashley, Directory of Defense Intelligence Agency). Retrieved from https://www.dia.mil/News/Speeches-and-Testimonies/Article-View/Article/1457815/statement-for-the-record-worldwide-threat-assessment/.

Verizon. (2018a). 2018 Data Breach Investigative Report. Retrieved from https://enterprise.verizon.com/resources/reports/DBIR_2018_Report.pdf.

Verizon. (2018b). 2018 Data Breach Investigative Report. Retrieved from https://enterprise.verizon.com/resources/reports/DBIR_2018_Report.pdf.

Visser, S. (2016). 5 Disruptive Technologies That are Challenging the Traditional Banking Model. Retrieved from https://www.ibmbigdatahub.com/blog/5-disruptive-technologies-are-challenging-traditional-banking-model.

Ward, J. S., & Barker, A. (2013). Undefined By Data: A Survey of Big Data Definitions. Retrieved from https://arxiv.org/abs/1309.5821.

Weill, P., & Ross, J. W. (2009). *IT Savvy: What Top Executives Must Know to Go from Pain to Gain.* Harvard Business Press.

World Bank Group. (2017). Good Practices for Consumer Marketing. Retrieved from https://www.worldbank.org/en/topic/financialinclusion/brief/2017-good-practices-for-financial-consumer-protection.

World Economic Forum. (2015). The Future of Financial Services. Retrieved from http://www3.weforum.org/docs/WEF_The_future__of_financial_services.pdf.

World Internet Usage—Nielsen Online and International Telecommunication Union. Retrieved from https://www.internetworldstats.com/stats.htm.

World Summit on the Information Society—Geneva 2003—Tunis 2005. Retrieved from https://www.itu.int/net/wsis/basic/about.html.

Index

V. C. Joshi, *Digital Finance, Bits and Bytes*,
https://doi.org/10.1007/978-981-15-3431-7

The manufacturer's authorised representative in the EU is Springer Nature Customer Service Centre GmbH, Europaplatz 3, 69115 Heidelberg, Germany. If you have any concerns regarding our products, please contact ProductSafety@springernature.com

Printed and bound by CPI Group (UK) Ltd, Croydon, CR0 4YY
25/09/2026
02222902-0002